John Ruskin

Munera Pulveris

Six Essays on the Elements of Political Economy

John Ruskin

Munera Pulveris

Six Essays on the Elements of Political Economy

ISBN/EAN: 9783337134242

Printed in Europe, USA, Canada, Australia, Japan

Cover: Foto ©Suzi / pixelio.de

More available books at **www.hansebooks.com**

MUNERA PULVERIS

SIX ESSAYS

ON THE ELEMENTS OF

POLITICAL ECONOMY.

BY

JOHN RUSKIN,

HONORARY STUDENT OF CHRIST CHURCH, AND HONORARY FELLOW
OF CORPUS CHRISTI COLLEGE, OXFORD.

SECOND SMALL EDITION.

GEORGE ALLEN, SUNNYSIDE, ORPINGTON,

AND

156, CHARING CROSS ROAD, LONDON.

1894.

[*All rights reserved.*]

CONTENTS

	PAGE
PREFACE	vii

CHAP.		
I.	DEFINITIONS	1
II.	STORE-KEEPING	27
III.	COIN-KEEPING	76
IV.	COMMERCE	110
V.	GOVERNMENT	129
VI.	MASTERSHIP	173

APPENDICES	207
INDEX	219

PREFACE

1. The following pages contain, I believe, the first accurate analysis of the laws of Political Economy which has been published in England. Many treatises, within their scope, correct, have appeared in contradiction of the views popularly received; but no exhaustive examination of the subject was possible to any person unacquainted with the value of the products of the highest industries, commonly called the "Fine Arts;" and no one acquainted with the nature of those industries has, so far as I know, attempted, or even approached, the task.

So that, to the date (1863) when these Essays were published, not only the chief conditions of the production of wealth had remained unstated, but the nature of wealth itself had never been defined. "Every one has a notion, sufficiently correct for common purposes, of what is meant by wealth," wrote Mr. Mill, in the outset of his treatise; and contentedly proceeded, as if a chemist should proceed to investigate the laws of chemistry without endeavouring to ascertain the nature of fire or water, because every one had a notion of them, "sufficiently correct for common purposes."

2. But even that apparently indisputable statement was untrue. There is not one person in ten thousand who has a notion sufficiently correct, even for the commonest purposes, of "what is meant" by wealth; still less of what wealth everlastingly *is*, whether we mean it or not; which it is the business of every student of economy to ascertain. We, indeed, know (either by experience or in imagination) what it is to be able to provide ourselves with luxurious food, and handsome clothes; and if Mr. Mill had thought that wealth consisted only in these, or in the means of obtaining these, it would have been easy for him to have so defined it with perfect scientific accuracy. But he knew better: he knew that some kinds of wealth consisted in

the possession, or power of obtaining, other things than these; but, having, in the studies of his life, no clue to the principles of essential value, he was compelled to take public opinion as the ground of his science; and the public, of course, willingly accepted the notion of a science founded on their opinions.

3. I had, on the contrary, a singular advantage, not only in the greater extent of the field of investigation opened to me by my daily pursuits, but in the severity of some lessons I accidentally received in the course of them.

When, in the winter of 1851, I was collecting materials for my work on Venetian architecture, three of the pictures of Tintoret on the roof of the School of St. Roch were hanging down in ragged fragments, mixed with lath and plaster, round the apertures made by the fall of three Austrian heavy shot. The city of Venice was not, it appeared, rich enough to repair the damage that winter; and buckets were set on the floor of the upper room of the school to catch the rain, which not only fell directly through the shot holes, but found its way, owing to the generally pervious state of the roof, through many of the canvases of Tintoret in other parts of the ceiling.

4. It was a lesson to me, as I have just said, no less direct than severe; for I knew already at that time (though I have not ventured to assert, until recently at Oxford,) that the pictures of Tintoret in Venice were accurately the most precious articles of wealth in Europe, being the best existing productions of human industry. Now at the time that three of them were thus fluttering in moist rags from the roof they had adorned, the shops of the Rue Rivoli at Paris were, in obedience to a steadily-increasing public Demand, beginning to show a steadily-increasing Supply of elaborately finished and coloured lithographs, representing the modern dances of delight, among which the cancan has since taken a distinguished place.

5. The labour employed on the stone of one of these lithographs is very much more than Tintoret was in the habit of giving to a picture of average size. Considering labour as the origin of value, therefore, the stone so highly wrought would be of greater value than the picture; and since also it is capable of

producing a large number of immediately saleable or exchangeable impressions, for which the "demand" is constant, the city of Paris naturally supposed itself, and on all hitherto believed or stated principles of political economy, was, infinitely richer in the possession of a large number of these lithographic stones, (not to speak of countless oil pictures and marble carvings of similar character), than Venice in the possession of those rags of mildewed canvas, flaunting in the south wind and its salt rain. And, accordingly, Paris provided (without thought of the expense) lofty arcades of shops, and rich recesses of innumerable private apartments, for the protection of these better treasures of hers from the weather.

6. Yet, all the while, Paris was not the richer for these possessions. Intrinsically, the delightful lithographs were not wealth, but polar contraries of wealth. She was, by the exact quantity of labour she had given to produce these, sunk below, instead of above, absolute Poverty. They not only were false Riches—they were true *Debt* which had to be paid at last—and the present aspect of the Rue Rivoli shows in what manner.

And the faded stains of the Venetian ceiling, all the while, were absolute and inestimable wealth. Useless to their possessors as forgotten treasure in a buried city, they had in them, nevertheless, the intrinsic and eternal nature of wealth; and Venice, still possessing the ruins of them, was a rich city; only, the Venetians had *not* a notion sufficiently correct even for tne very common purpose of inducing them to put slates on a roof, of what was "meant by wealth."

7. The vulgar economist would reply that his science had nothing to do with the qualities of pictures, but with their exchange-value only; and that his business was, exclusively, to consider whether the remains of Tintoret were worth as many ten-and-sixpences as the impressions which might be taken from the lithographic stones.

But he would not venture, without reserve, to make such an answer, if the example be taken in horses, instead of pictures. The most dull economist would perceive, and admit, that a gentleman who had a fine stud of horses was absolutely richer than one who had only ill-bred and broken-winded ones. He would instinctively feel, though his pseudo-science had never taught him, that the price paid for the animals, in either case, did not alter the fact of their worth; that the good horse, though it might have been bought by chance for a few guineas, was not therefore less valuable, nor the owner of the galled jade any the richer, because he had given a hundred for it.

8. So that the economist, in saying that his science takes no account of the qualities of pictures, merely signifies that he cannot conceive of any quality of essential badness or goodness existing in pictures; and that he is incapable of investigating the laws of wealth in such articles. Which is the fact. But, being incapable of defining intrinsic value in pictures, it follows that he must be equally helpless to define the nature of intrinsic value in painted glass, or in painted pottery, or in patterned stuffs, or in any other national produce requiring true human ingenuity. Nay, though capable of conceiving the idea of intrinsic value with respect to beasts of burden, no economist has endeavoured to state the general principles of National Economy, even

with regard to the horse or the ass. And, in fine, *the modern political economists have been, without exception, incapable of apprehending the nature of intrinsic value at all.*

9. And the first specialty of the following treatise consists in its giving at the outset, and maintaining as the foundation of all subsequent reasoning, a definition of Intrinsic Value, and Intrinsic Contrary-of-Value; the negative power having been left by former writers entirely out of account, and the positive power left entirely undefined.

But, secondly: the modern economist, ignoring intrinsic value, and accepting the popular estimate of things as the only ground of his science, has imagined himself to have ascertained the constant laws regulating the relation of this popular demand to its supply; or, at least, to have proved that demand and supply were connected by heavenly balance, over which human foresight had no power. I chanced, by singular coincidence, lately to see this theory of the law of demand and supply brought to as sharp practical issue in another great siege, as I had seen the theories of intrinsic value brought, in the siege of Venice.

10. I had the honour of being on the committee under the presidentship of the Lord Mayor of London, for the victualling of Paris after her surrender. It became, at one period of our sittings, a question of vital importance at what moment the law of demand and supply would come into operation, and what the operation of it would exactly be: the demand on this occasion, being very urgent indeed; that of several millions of people within a few hours of utter starvation, for any kind of food whatsoever. Nevertheless, it was admitted, in the course of debate, to be probable that the divine principle of demand and supply might find itself at the eleventh hour, and some minutes over, in want of carts and horses; and we ventured so far to interfere with the divine principle as to provide carts and horses, with haste which proved, happily, in time for the need; but not a moment in advance of it. It was farther recognised by the committee that the divine principle of demand and supply would commence its operations by charging the poor of Paris twelve-pence for a penny's worth of whatever they wanted; and would end its

operations by offering them twelve-pence worth for a penny, of whatever they didn't want. Whereupon it was concluded by the committee that the tiny knot, on this special occasion, was scarcely "*dignus vindice*," by the divine principle of demand and supply : and that we would venture, for once, in a profane manner, to provide for the poor of Paris what they wanted, when they wanted it. Which, to the value of the sums entrusted to us, it will be remembered we succeeded in doing.

11. But the fact is that the so-called "Law," which was felt to be false in this case of extreme exigence, is alike false in cases of less exigence. It is false always, and everywhere. Nay, to such an extent is its existence imaginary, that the vulgar economists are not even agreed in their account of it; for some of them mean by it, only that prices are regulated by the relation between demand and supply, which is partly true; and others mean that the relation itself is one with the process of which it is unwise to interfere; a statement which is not only, as in the above instance, untrue; but accurately the reverse of the truth: for all wise economy, political

or domestic, consists in the resolved maintenance of a given relation between supply and demand, other than the instinctive, or (directly) natural, one.

12. Similarly, vulgar political economy asserts for a "law" that wages are determined by competition.

Now I pay my servants exactly what wages I think necessary to make them comfortable. The sum is not determined at all by competition; but sometimes by my notions of their comfort and deserving, and sometimes by theirs. If I were to become penniless tomorrow, several of them would certainly still serve me for nothing.

In both the real and supposed cases the so-called "law" of vulgar political economy is absolutely set at defiance. But I cannot set the law of gravitation at defiance, nor determine that in my house I will not allow ice to melt, when the temperature is above thirty-two degrees. A true law outside of my house, will remain a true one inside of it. It is not, therefore, a law of Nature that wages are determined by competition. Still less is it a law of State, or we should not now

b

be disputing about it publicly, to the loss of many millions of pounds to the country. The fact which vulgar economists have been weak enough to imagine a law, is only that, for the last twenty years a number of very senseless persons have attempted to determine wages in that manner; and have, in a measure, succeeded in occasionally doing so.

13. Both in definition of the elements of wealth, and in statement of the laws which govern its distribution, modern political economy has been thus absolutely incompetent, or absolutely false. And the following treatise is not as it has been asserted with dull pertinacity, an endeavour to put sentiment in the place of science; but it contains the exposure of what insolently pretended to be a science; and the definition, hitherto unassailed—and I do not fear to assert, unassailable—of the material elements with which political economy has to deal, and the moral principles in which it consists; being not itself a science, but "a system of conduct founded on the sciences, and impossible, except under certain conditions of moral culture." Which is only to say, that industry, frugality, and discretion,

the three foundations of economy, are moral qualities, and cannot be attained without moral discipline: a flat truism, the reader may think, thus stated, yet a truism which is denied both vociferously, and in all endeavour, by the entire populace of Europe; who are at present hopeful of obtaining wealth by tricks of trade, without industry; who, possessing wealth, have lost in the use of it even the conception,—how much more the habit?—of frugality; and who, in the choice of the elements of wealth, cannot so much as lose—since they have never hitherto at any time possessed,—the faculty of discretion.

14. Now if the teachers of the pseudo-science of economy had ventured to state distinctly even the poor conclusions they had reached on the subjects respecting which it is most dangerous for a populace to be indiscreet, they would have soon found, by the use made of them, which were true, and which false.

But on main and vital questions, no political economist has hitherto ventured to state one guiding principle. I will instance three subjects of universal importance. National Dress. National Rent. National Debt.

Now if we are to look in any quarter for a systematic and exhaustive statement of the principles of a given science, it must certainly be from its Professor at Cambridge.

15. Take the last edition of Professor Fawcett's *Manual of Political Economy*, and forming, first, clearly in your mind these three following questions, see if you can find an answer to them.

I. Does expenditure of capital on the production of luxurious dress and furniture tend to make a nation rich or poor?

II. Does the payment, by the nation, of a tax on its land, or on the produce of it, to a certain number of private persons, to be expended by them as they please, tend to make the nation rich or poor?

III. Does the payment, by the nation, for an indefinite period, of interest on money borrowed from private persons, tend to make the nation rich or poor?

These three questions are, all of them, perfectly simple, and primarily vital. Determine these, and you have at once a basis for national conduct in all important particulars. Leave them undetermined, and there is no limit to the distress which may be brought upon the people by the cunning of its knaves, and the folly of its multitudes.

I will take the three in their order.

16. (I.) Dress. The general impression on the public mind at this day is, that the luxury of the rich in dress and furniture is a benefit to the poor. Probably not even the blindest of our political economists would venture to assert this in so many words. But where do they assert the contrary? During the entire period of the reign of the late Emperor it was assumed in France, as the first principle of fiscal government, that a large portion of the funds received as rent from the provincial labourer should be expended in the manufacture of ladies' dresses in Paris. Where is the political economist in France, or England, who ventured to assert the conclusions of his science as adverse to this system? As early as the year 1857 I had done my best to show the nature of the error, and to give warning of its danger;* but not one of the men who had the foolish ears of the people intent on

---

* *Political Economy of Art.* (Now "A Joy for Ever,"—Vol. XI. of the Revised Series of Entire Works.—pp. 47 56.)

their words, dared to follow me in speaking what would have been an offence to the powers of trade; and the powers of trade in Paris had their full way for fourteen years more,—with this result, to-day,—as told us in precise and curt terms by the Minister of Public Instruction,*—

"We have replaced glory by gold, work by speculation, faith and honour by scepticism. To absolve or glorify immorality; to make much of loose women; to gratify our eyes with luxury, our ears with the tales of orgies; to aid in the manœuvres of public robbers, or to applaud them; to laugh at morality, and only believe in success; to love nothing but pleasure, adore nothing but force; to replace work with a fecundity of fancies; to speak without thinking; to prefer noise to glory; to erect sneering into a system, and lying into an institution—is this the spectacle that we have seen?—is this the society that we have been?"

Of course, other causes, besides the desire of luxury in furniture and dress, have been at work to produce such consequences; but the most active cause of all has been the passion

* See report of speech of M. Jules Simon, in *Pall Mall Gazette* of October 27th, 1871.

for these; passion unrebuked by the clergy, and, for the most part, provoked by economists, as advantageous to commerce; nor need we think that such results have been arrived at in France only; we are ourselves following rapidly on the same road. France, in her old wars with us, never was so fatally our enemy as she has been in the fellowship of fashion, and the freedom of trade: nor, to my mind, is any fact recorded of Assyrian or Roman luxury more ominous, or ghastly, than one which came to my knowledge a few weeks ago, in England; a respectable and well-to-do father and mother, in a quiet north country town, being turned into the streets in their old age, at the suit of their only daughter's milliner.

17. (II.) Rent. The following account of the real nature of rent is given, quite accurately, by Professor Fawcett, at page 112 of the last edition of his *Political Economy*:—

"Every country has probably been subjugated, and grants of vanquished territory were the ordinary rewards which the conquering chief bestowed upon his more distinguished followers. Lands obtained by force had to be defended by force;

and before law had asserted her supremacy, and property was made secure, no baron was able to retain his possessions, unless those who lived on his estates were prepared to defend them. . . .* As property became secure, and landlords felt that the power of the State would protect them in all the rights of property, every vestige of these feudal tenures was abolished, and the relation between landlord and tenant has thus become purely commercial. A landlord offers his land to any one who is willing to take it; he is anxious to receive the highest rent he can obtain. What are the principles which regulate the rent which may thus be paid?"

These principles the Professor goes on contentedly to investigate, never appearing to contemplate for an instant the possibility of the first principle in the whole business—the maintenance, by force, of the possession of land obtained by force, being ever called in question by any human mind. It is, nevertheless, the nearest task of our day to discover how far original theft may be justly encountered by reactionary theft, or whether reactionary theft be indeed theft at all; and

---

* The omitted sentences merely amplify the statement: they in no wise modify it.

farther, what, excluding either original or corrective theft, are the just conditions of the possession of land.

18. (III.) Debt. Long since, when, a mere boy, I used to sit silently listening to the conversation of the London merchants who, all of them good and sound men of business, were wont occasionally to meet round my father's dining-table, nothing used to surprise me more than the conviction openly expressed by some of the soundest and most cautious of them, that "if there were no National debt they would not know what to do with their money, or where to place it safely." At the 399th page of his Manual, you will find Professor Fawcett giving exactly the same statement.

"In our own country, this certainty against risk of loss is provided by the public funds;"

and again, as on the question of rent, the Professor proceeds, without appearing for an instant to be troubled by any misgiving that there may be an essential difference between the effects on national prosperity of a Government paying interest on money which it spent in fireworks fifty years ago, and of a Government paying interest on money to be employed to-day on productive labour.

That difference, which the reader will find stated and examined at length, in §§ 127–129 of this volume, it is the business of economists, before approaching any other question relating to government, fully to explain. And the paragraphs to which I refer, contain, I believe, the only definite statement of it hitherto made.

19. The practical result of the absence of any such statement is, that capitalists, when they do not know what to do with their money, persuade the peasants, in various countries, that the said peasants want guns to shoot each other with. The peasants accordingly borrow guns, out of the manufacture of which the capitalists get a per-centage, and men of science much amusement and credit. Then the peasants shoot a certain number of each other, until they get tired; and burn each other's homes down in various places. Then they put the guns back into towers, arsenals, etc., in ornamental patterns; (and the victorious party put also some ragged flags in churches). And then the capitalists tax both, annually,

ever afterwards, to pay interest on the loan of the guns and gunpowder. And that is what capitalists call "knowing what to do with their money;" and what commercial men in general call "practical" as opposed to "sentimental" Political Economy.

20. Eleven years ago, in the summer of 1860, perceiving then fully, (as Carlyle had done long before), what distress was about to come on the said populace of Europe through these errors of their teachers, I began to do the best I might, to combat them, in the series of papers for the *Cornhill Magazine*, since published under the title of *Unto this Last*. The editor of the Magazine was my friend, and ventured the insertion of the three first essays; but the outcry against them became then too strong for any editor to endure, and he wrote to me, with great discomfort to himself, and many apologies to me, that the Magazine must only admit one Economical Essay more.

I made, with his permission, the last one longer than the rest, and gave it blunt conclusion as well as I could—and so the book now stands; but, as I had taken not a little pains with the Essays, and knew that they contained better work than most of my former writings, and more important truths than all of them put together, this violent reprobation of them by the *Cornhill* public set me still more gravely thinking; and, after turning the matter hither and thither in my mind for two years more, I resolved to make it the central work of my life to write an exhaustive treatise on Political Economy. It would not have been begun, at that time, however, had not the editor of *Fraser's Magazine* written to me, saying that he believed there was something in my theories, and would risk the admission of what I chose to write on this dangerous subject; whereupon, cautiously, and at intervals, during the winter of 1862–63, I sent him, and he ventured to print, the preface of the intended work, divided into four chapters. Then, though the Editor had not wholly lost courage, the Publisher indignantly interfered; and the readers of *Fraser*, as those of the *Cornhill*, were protected, for that time, from farther disturbance on my part. Subsequently, loss of health, family distress, and various untoward chances, prevented my proceeding with the body of the book;—seven years have passed ineffectually; and I am now fain to reprint the Preface by itself, under the title which I intended for the whole.

21. Not discontentedly; being, at this time of life, resigned to the sense of failure; and also, because the preface is complete in itself as a body of definitions, which I now require for reference in the course of my *Letters to Workmen;* by which also, in time, I trust less formally to accomplish the chief purpose of *Munera Pulveris* practically summed in the two paragraphs 27 and 28: namely, to examine the moral results and possible rectifications of the laws of distribution of wealth, which have prevailed hitherto without debate among men. Laws which ordinary economists assume to be inviolable, and which ordinary socialists imagine to be on the eve of total abrogation. But they are both alike deceived. The laws which at present regulate the possession of wealth are unjust, because the motives which provoke to its attainment are impure; but no socialism can effect their abrogation, unless it can abrogate also covetousness and pride, which it is by no means yet in the way of doing. Nor can the change be, in any

case, to the extent that has been imagined. Extremes of luxury may be forbidden, and agony of penury relieved; but nature intends, and the utmost efforts of socialism will not hinder the fulfilment of her intention, that a provident person shall always be richer than a spendthrift; and an ingenious one more comfortable than a fool. But, indeed, the adjustment of the possession of the products of industry depends more on their nature than their quantity, and on wise determination therefore of the aims of industry. A nation which desires true wealth, desires it moderately, and can therefore distribute it with kindness, and possess it with pleasure; but one which desires false wealth, desires it immoderately, and can neither dispense it with justice, nor enjoy it in peace.

22. Therefore, needing, constantly in my present work, to refer to the definitions of true and false wealth given in the following Essays, I republish them with careful revisal. They were written abroad; partly at Milan, partly during a winter residence on the south-eastern slope of the Mont Salève, near Geneva; and sent to London in as legible MS. as I could

write; but I never revised the press sheets, and have been obliged, accordingly, now to amend the text here and there, or correct it in unimportant particulars. Wherever any modification has involved change in the sense, it is enclosed in square brackets; and what few explanatory comments I have felt it necessary to add, have been indicated in the same manner. No explanatory comments, I regret to perceive, will suffice to remedy the mischief of my affected concentration of language, into the habit of which I fell by thinking too long over particular passages, in many and many a solitary walk towards the mountains of Bonneville or Annecy. But I never intended the book for anything else than a dictionary of reference, and that for earnest readers; who will, I have good hope, if they find what they want in it, forgive the affectedly curt expressions.

The Essays, as originally published, were, as I have just stated, four in number. I have now, more conveniently, divided the whole into six chapters; and (as I purpose throughout this edition of my works) numbered the paragraphs.

I inscribed the first volume of this series to the friend who aided me in chief sorrow. Let me inscribe the second to the friend and guide who has urged me to all chief labour, THOMAS CARLYLE.

23. I would that some better means were in my power of showing reverence to the man who alone, of all our masters of literature, has written, without thought of himself, what he knew it to be needful for the people of his time to hear, if the will to hear were in them: whom, therefore, as the time draws near when his task must be ended, Republican and Free-thoughted England assaults with impatient reproach; and out of the abyss of her cowardice in policy and dishonour in trade, sets the hacks of her literature to speak evil, grateful to her ears, of the Solitary Teacher who has asked her to be brave for the help of Man, and just, for the love of God.

DENMARK HILL,
25th November, 1871.

MUNERA PULVERIS

"TE MARIS ET TERRÆ NUMEROQUE CARENTIS ARENÆ
   MENSOREM COHIBENT, ARCHYTA,
PULVERIS EXIGUI PROPE LITUS PARVA MATINUM
   MUNERA."

CHAPTER I.

DEFINITIONS.

1. As domestic economy regulates the acts and habits of a household, Political Economy regulates those of a society or State, with reference to the means of its maintenance.

Political economy is neither an art nor a science; but a system of conduct and legislature, founded on the sciences, directing the arts, and impossible, except under certain conditions of moral culture.

2. The study which lately in England has been called Political Economy is in reality nothing more than the investigation of some

accidental phenomena of modern commercial operations, nor has it been true in its investigation even of these. It has no connection whatever with political economy, as understood and treated of by the great thinkers of past ages; and as long as its unscholarly and undefined statements are allowed to pass under the same name, every word written on the subject by those thinkers—and chiefly the words of Plato, Xenophon, Cicero, and Bacon—must be nearly useless to mankind. The reader must not, therefore, be surprised at the care and insistance with which I have retained the literal and earliest sense of all important terms used in these papers; for a word is usually well made at the time it is first wanted; its youngest meaning has in it the full strength of its youth; subsequent senses are commonly warped or weakened; and as all careful thinkers are sure to have used their words accurately, the first condition, in order to be able to avail ourselves of their sayings at all, is firm definition of terms.

3. By the "maintenance" of a State is to be understood the support of its population in healthy and happy life; and the increase of

their numbers, so far as that increase is consistent with their happiness. It is not the object of political economy to increase the numbers of a nation at the cost of common health or comfort; nor to increase indefinitely the comfort of individuals, by sacrifice of surrounding lives, or possibilities of life.

4. The assumption which lies at the root of nearly all erroneous reasoning on political economy,—namely, that its object is to accumulate money or exchangeable property,—may be shown in a few words to be without foundation. For no economist would admit national economy to be legitimate which proposed to itself only the building of a pyramid of gold. He would declare the gold to be wasted, were it to remain in the monumental form, and would say it ought to be employed. But to what end? Either it must be used only to gain more gold, and build a larger pyramid, or for some purpose other than the gaining of gold. And this other purpose, however at first apprehended, will be found to resolve itself finally into the service of man;—that is to say, the extension, defence, or comfort of his life. The golden pyramid may perhaps be

providently built, perhaps improvidently; but the wisdom or folly of the accumulation can only be determined by our having first clearly stated the aim of all economy, namely, the extension of life.

If the accumulation of money, or of exchangeable property, were a certain means of extending existence, it would be useless, in discussing economical questions, to fix our attention upon the more distant object—life—instead of the immediate one—money. But it is not so. Money may sometimes be accumulated at the cost of life, or by limitations of it; that is to say, either by hastening the deaths of men, or preventing their births. It is therefore necessary to keep clearly in view the ultimate object of economy; and to determine the expediency of minor operations with reference to that ulterior end.

5. It has been just stated that the object of political economy is the continuance not only of life, but of healthy and happy life. But all true happiness is both a consequence and cause of life: it is a sign of its vigour, and source of its continuance. All true suffering is in like manner a consequence and cause of death. I

shall therefore, in future, use the word "Life" singly : but let it be understood to include in its signification the happiness and power of the entire human nature, body and soul.

6. That human nature, as its Creator made it, and maintains it wherever His laws are observed, is entirely harmonious. No physical error can be more profound, no moral error more dangerous, than that involved in the monkish doctrine of the opposition of body to soul. No soul can be perfect in an imperfect body : no body perfect without perfect soul. Every right action and true thought sets the seal of its beauty on person and face; every wrong action and foul thought its seal of distortion; and the various aspects of humanity might be read as plainly as a printed history, were it not that the impressions are so complex that it must always in some cases (and, in the present state of our knowledge, in all cases) be impossible to decipher them completely. Nevertheless, the face of a consistently just, and of a consistently unjust person, may always be rightly distinguished at a glance ; and if the qualities are continued by descent through a generation or two, there

arises a complete distinction of race. Both moral and physical qualities are communicated by descent, far more than they can be developed by education, (though both may be destroyed by want of education); and there is as yet no ascertained limit to the nobleness of person and mind which the human creature may attain, by persevering observance of the laws of God respecting its birth and training.

7. We must therefore yet farther define the aim of political economy to be "The multiplication of human life at the highest standard." It might at first seem questionable whether we should endeavour to maintain a small number of persons of the highest type of beauty and intelligence, or a larger number of an inferior class. But I shall be able to show in the sequel, that the way to maintain the largest number is first to aim at the highest standard. Determine the noblest type of man, and aim simply at maintaining the largest possible number of persons of that class, and it will be found that the largest possible number of every healthy subordinate class must necessarily be produced also.

8. The perfect type of manhood, as just

stated, involves the perfections (whatever we may hereafter determine these to be) of his body, affections, and intelligence. The material things, therefore, which it is the object of political economy to produce and use, (or accumulate for use,) are things which serve either to sustain and comfort the body, or exercise rightly the affections and form the intelligence.* Whatever truly serves either of these purposes is "useful" to man, wholesome, healthful, helpful, or holy. By seeking such things, man prolongs and increases his life upon the earth.

On the other hand, whatever does not serve either of these purposes,—much more whatever counteracts them,—is in like manner useless to man, unwholesome, unhelpful, or unholy; and by seeking such things man shortens and diminishes his life upon the earth.

9. And neither with respect to things useful or useless can man's estimate of them alter their nature. Certain substances being good for his food, and others noxious to him, what he thinks or wishes respecting them can neither change, nor prevent, their power. If

* *See* Appendix I.

he eats corn, he will live; if nightshade, he will die. If he produce or make good and beautiful things, they will *Re-Create* him; (note the solemnity and weight of the word); if bad and ugly things, they will "corrupt" or "break in pieces"—that is, in the exact degree of their power, Kill him. For every hour of labour, however enthusiastic or well intended, which he spends for that which is not bread, so much possibility of life is lost to him. His fancies, likings, beliefs, however brilliant, eager, or obstinate, are of no avail if they are set on a false object. Of all that he has laboured for, the eternal law of heaven and earth measures out to him for reward, to the utmost atom, that part which he ought to have laboured for, and withdraws from him (or enforces on him, it may be) inexorably, that part which he ought not to have laboured for until, on his summer threshing-floor, stands his heap of corn; little or much, not according to his labour, but to his discretion. No "commercial arrangements," no painting of surfaces, nor alloying of substances, will avail him a pennyweight. Nature asks of him calmly and inevitably, What have you found, or formed—the right thing or the wrong? By the right thing you shall live; by the wrong you shall die.

10. To thoughtless persons it seems otherwise. The world looks to them as if they could cozen it out of some ways and means of life. But they cannot cozen IT: they can only cozen their neighbours. The world is not to be cheated of a grain; not so much as a breath of its air can be drawn surreptitiously. For every piece of wise work done, so much life is granted; for every piece of foolish work, nothing; for every piece of wicked work, so much death is allotted. This is as sure as the courses of day and night. But when the means of life are once produced, men, by their various struggles and industries of accumulation or exchange, may variously gather, waste, restrain, or distribute them; necessitating, in proportion to the waste or restraint, accurately, so much more death. The rate and range of additional death are measured by the rate and range of waste, and are inevitable;—the only question (determined mostly by fraud in peace, and force in war) is, Who is to die, and how?

11. Such being the everlasting law of human existence, the essential work of the political economist is to determine what are in reality useful or life-giving things, and by what degrees and kinds of labour they are attainable and distributable. This investigation divides itself under three great heads;—the studies, namely, of the phenomena, first, of WEALTH; secondly, of MONEY; and thirdly, of RICHES.

These terms are often used as synonymous, but they signify entirely different things. "Wealth" consists of things in themselves valuable; "Money," of documentary claims to the possession of such things; and "Riches" is a relative term, expressing the magnitude of the possessions of one person or society as compared with those of other persons or societies.

The study of Wealth is a province of natural science:—it deals with the essential properties of things.

The study of Money is a province of commercial science:—it deals with conditions of engagement and exchange.

The study of Riches is a province of moral

science:—it deals with the due relations of men to each other in regard of material possessions; and with the just laws of their association for purposes of labour.

I shall in this first chapter shortly sketch out the range of subjects which will come before us as we follow these three branches of inquiry.

12. And first of WEALTH, which, it has been said, consists of things essentially valuable. We now, therefore, need a definition of "value."

"Value" signifies the strength, or "availing" of anything towards the sustaining of life, and is always twofold; that is to say, primarily, INTRINSIC, and secondarily, EFFECTUAL.

The reader must, by anticipation, be warned against confusing value with cost, or with price. *Value is the life-giving power of anything; cost, the quantity of labour required to produce it; price, the quantity of labour which its possessor will take in exchange for it.** Cost

[* Observe these definitions,—they are of much importance,—and connect with them the sentences in italics on next page.]

and price are commercial conditions, to be studied under the head of money.

13. Intrinsic value is the absolute power of anything to support life. A sheaf of wheat of given quality and weight has in it a measurable power of sustaining the substance of the body; a cubic foot of pure air, a fixed power of sustaining its warmth; and a cluster of flowers of given beauty a fixed power of enlivening or animating the senses and heart.

It does not in the least affect the intrinsic value of the wheat, the air, or the flowers, that men refuse or despise them. Used or not, their own power is in them, and that particular power is in nothing else.

14. But in order that this value of theirs may become effectual, a certain state is necessary in the recipient of it. The digesting, breathing, and perceiving functions must be perfect in the human creature before the food, air, or flowers can become of their full value to it. *The production of effectual value, therefore, always involves two needs: first, the production of a thing essentially useful; then the production of the capacity to use it.* Where the intrinsic value and acceptant capacity come

together there is Effectual value, or wealth; where there is either no intrinsic value, or no acceptant capacity, there is no effectual value; that is to say, no wealth. A horse is no wealth to us if we cannot ride, nor a picture if we cannot see, *nor can any noble thing be wealth, except to a noble person.* As the aptness of the user increases, the effectual value of the thing used increases; and in its entirety can co-exist only with perfect skill of use, and fitness of nature.

15. Valuable material things may be conveniently referred to five heads:

(i.) Land, with its associated air, water, and organisms.

(ii.) Houses, furniture, and instruments.

(iii.) Stored or prepared food, medicine, and articles of bodily luxury, including clothing.

(iv.) Books.

(v.) Works of art.

The conditions of value in these things are briefly as follows:—

16. (i.) Land. Its value is twofold; first, as producing food and mechanical power; secondly, as an object of sight and thought, producing intellectual power.

Its value, as a means of producing food and mechanical power, varies with its form (as mountain or plain), with its substance (in soil or mineral contents), and with its climate. All these conditions of intrinsic value must be known and complied with by the men who have to deal with it, in order to give effectual value; but at any given time and place, the intrinsic value is fixed: such and such a piece of land, with its associated lakes and seas, rightly treated in surface and substance, can produce precisely so much food and power, and no more.

The second element of value in land being its beauty, united with such conditions of space and form as are necessary for exercise, and for fulness of animal life, land of the highest value in these respects will be that lying in temperate climates, and boldly varied in form; removed from unhealthy or dangerous influences (as of miasm or volcano); and capable of sustaining a rich fauna and flora. Such land, carefully tended by the hand of man, so far as to remove from it unsightlinesses and evidences of decay, guarded from violence, and inhabited, under man's affectionate protection, by every kind of living creature that can occupy it in peace, is the most precious "property" that human beings can possess.

17. (ii.) Buildings, furniture, and instruments.

The value of buildings consists, first, in permanent strength, with convenience of form, of size, and of position; so as to render employment peaceful, social intercourse easy, temperature and air healthy. The advisable or possible magnitude of cities and mode of their distribution in squares, streets, courts, etc.; the relative value of sites of land, and the modes of structure which are healthiest and most permanent, have to be studied under this head.

The value of buildings consists secondly in historical association, and architectural beauty, of which we have to examine the influence on manners and life.

The value of instruments consists, first, in their power of shortening labour, or otherwise accomplishing what human strength unaided could not. The kinds of work which are severally best accomplished by hand or by machine;—the effect of machinery in gathering and multiplying population, and its influence on the minds and bodies of such population; together with the conceivable uses of machinery on a colossal scale in accomplishing mighty and useful works, hitherto unthought of, such as the deepening of large river channels;—changing the surface of mountainous districts;—irrigating tracts of desert in the torrid zone;—breaking up, and thus rendering capable of quicker fusion, edges of ice in the northern and southern Arctic seas, etc., so rendering parts of the earth habitable which hitherto have been lifeless, are to be studied under this head.

The value of instruments is, secondarily, in their aid to abstract sciences. The degree in which the multiplication of such instruments should be encouraged, so as to make them, if large, easy of access to numbers (as costly telescopes), or so cheap as that they might, in a serviceable form, become a common part of the furniture of households, is to be considered under this head.*

---

* I cannot now recast these sentences, pedantic in their generalization, and intended more for index than statement, but I must guard the reader from thinking that I ever wish

18. (iii.) Food, medicine, and articles of luxury. Under this head we shall have to examine the possible methods of obtaining pure food in such security and equality of supply as to avoid both waste and famine: then the economy of medicine and just range of sanitary law : finally the economy of luxury, partly an æsthetic and partly an ethical question.

19. (iv.) Books. The value of these consists,

First, in their power of preserving and communicating the knowledge of facts.

Secondly, in their power of exciting vital or noble emotion and intellectual action. They have also their corresponding negative powers of disguising and effacing the memory of facts, and killing the noble emotions, or exciting base ones. Under these two heads we have to consider the economical and educational value, positive and negative, of literature ;—the means of producing and educating

for cheapness by bad quality. A poor boy need not always learn mathematics ; but, if you set him to do so, have the farther kindness to give him good compasses, not cheap ones, whose points bend like lead.]

good authors, and the means and advisability of rendering good books generally accessible, and directing the reader's choice to them.

20. (v.) Works of art. The value of these is of the same nature as that of books; but the laws of their production and possible modes of distribution are very different, and require separate examination.

21. II.—MONEY. Under this head, we shall have to examine the laws of currency and exchange; of which I will note here the first separate principles.

Money has been inaccurately spoken of as merely a means of exchange. But it is far more than this. It is a documentary expression of legal claim. It is not wealth, but a documentary claim to wealth, being the sign of the relative quantities of it, or of the labour producing it, to which, at a given time, persons, or societies, are entitled.

If all the money in the world, notes and gold, were destroyed in an instant, it would leave the world neither richer nor poorer than it was. But it would leave the individual inhabitants of it in different relations.

Money is, therefore, correspondent in its

nature to the title-deed of an estate. Though the deed be burned, the estate still exists, but the right to it has become disputable.

22. The real worth of money remains unchanged, as long as the proportion of the quantity of existing money to the quantity of existing wealth or available labour remains unchanged.

If the wealth increases, but not the money, the worth of the money increases; if the money increases, but not the wealth, the worth of the money diminishes.

23. Money, therefore, cannot be arbitrarily multiplied, any more than title-deeds can. So long as the existing wealth or available labour is not fully represented by the currency, the currency may be increased without diminution of the assigned worth of its pieces. But when the existing wealth, or available labour, is once fully represented, every piece of money thrown into circulation diminishes the worth of every other existing piece, in the proportion it bears to the number of them, provided the new piece be received with equal credit; if not, the depreciation of worth takes place, according to the degree of its credit.

24. When, however, new money, composed of some substance of supposed intrinsic value (as of gold), is brought into the market, or when new notes are issued which are supposed to be deserving of credit, the desire to obtain the money will, under certain circumstances, stimulate industry: an additional quantity of wealth is immediately produced, and if this be in proportion to the new claims advanced, the value of the existing currency is undepreciated. If the stimulus given be so great as to produce more goods than are proportioned to the additional coinage, the worth of the existing currency will be raised.

Arbitrary control and issues of currency affect the production of wealth, by acting on the hopes and fears of men, and are, under certain circumstances, wise. But the issue of additional currency to meet the exigencies of immediate expense, is merely one of the disguised forms of borrowing or taxing. It is, however, in the present low state of economical knowledge, often possible for governments to venture on an issue of currency, when they could not venture on an additional loan or tax, because the real operation of such issue is not understood by the people, and the pressure of it is irregularly distributed, and with an unperceived gradation.

25. The use of substances of intrinsic value as the materials of a currency, is a barbarism; —a remnant of the conditions of barter, which alone render commerce possible among savage nations. It is, however, still necessary, partly as a mechanical check on arbitrary issues; partly as a means of exchanges with foreign nations. In proportion to the extension of civilization, and increase of trustworthiness in governments, it will cease. So long as it exists, the phenomena of the cost and price of the articles used for currency are mingled with those proper to currency itself, in an almost inextricable manner: and the market worth of bullion is affected by multitudinous accidental circumstances, which have been traced, with more or less success, by writers on commercial operations: but with these variations the true political economist has no more to do than an engineer, fortifying a harbour of refuge against Atlantic tide, has to concern himself with the cries or quarrels of children who dig pools with their fingers for its streams among the sand.

26. III.—RICHES. According to the various industry, capacity, good fortune, and desires of men, they obtain greater or smaller share of, and claim upon, the wealth of the world.

The inequalities between these shares, always in some degree just and necessary, may be either restrained by law or circumstance within certain limits; or may increase indefinitely.

Where no moral or legal restraint is put upon the exercise of the will and intellect of the stronger, shrewder, or more covetous men, these differences become ultimately enormous. But as soon as they become so distinct in their extremes as that, on one side, there shall be manifest redundance of possession, and on the other manifest pressure of need,—the terms "riches" and "poverty" are used to express the opposite states; being contrary only as the terms "warmth" and "cold" are contraries, of which neither implies an actual degree, but only a relation to other degrees, of temperature.

27. Respecting riches, the economist has to inquire, first, into the advisable modes of their collection; secondly, into the advisable modes of their administration.

Respecting the collection of national riches, he has to inquire, first, whether he is justified in calling the nation rich, if the quantity of wealth it possesses relatively to the wealth of other nations, be large; irrespectively of the manner of its distribution. Or does the mode of distribution in any wise affect the nature of the riches? Thus, if the king alone be rich—suppose Crœsus or Mausolus—are the Lydians or Carians therefore a rich nation? Or if a few slave-masters are rich, and the nation is otherwise composed of slaves, is it to be called a rich nation? For if not, and the ideas of a certain mode of distribution or operation in the riches, and of a certain degree of freedom in the people, enter into our idea of riches as attributed to a people, we shall have to define the degree of fluency, or circulative character which is essential to the nature of common wealth; and the degree of independence of action required in its possessors. Questions which look as if they would take time in answering.*

28. And farther. Since the inequality, which

[* I regret the ironical manner in which this passage, one of great importance in the matter of it, was written. The gist of it is, that the first of all inquiries respecting the

is the condition of riches, may be established in two opposite modes—namely, by increase of possession on the one side, and by decrease of it on the other—we have to inquire, with respect to any given state of riches, precisely in what manner the correlative poverty was produced: that is to say, whether by being surpassed only, or being depressed also; and if by being depressed, what are the advantages, or the contrary, conceivable in the depression. For instance, it being one of the commonest advantages of being rich to entertain a number of servants, we have to inquire, on the one side, what economical process produced the riches of the master; and on the other, what economical process produced the poverty of the persons who serve him; and what advantages each, on his own side, derives from the result.

29. These being the main questions touching the collection of riches, the next, or last, part of the inquiry is into their administration.

Their possession involves three great economical powers which require separate

wealth of any nation is not, how much it has; but whether it is in a form that can be used, and in the possession of persons who can use it.]

examination: namely, the powers of selection, direction, and provision.

The power of SELECTION relates to things of which the supply is limited (as the supply of best things is always). When it becomes matter of question to whom such things are to belong, the richest person has necessarily the first choice, unless some arbitrary mode of distribution be otherwise determined upon. The business of the economist is to show how this choice may be a Wise one.

The power of DIRECTION arises out of the necessary relation of rich men to poor, which ultimately, in one way or another, involves the direction of, or authority over, the labour of the poor; and this nearly as much over their mental as their bodily labour. The business of the economist is to show how this direction may be a Just one.

The power of PROVISION is dependent upon the redundance of wealth, which may of course by active persons be made available in preparation for future work or future profit; in which function riches have generally received the name of capital; that is to say, of head-, or source-material. The business of the economist is to show how this provision may be a Distant one.

30. The examination of these three functions of riches will embrace every final problem of political economy;—and, above, or before all, this curious and vital problem,—whether, since the wholesome action of riches in these three functions will depend (it appears) on the Wisdom, Justice, and Farsightedness of the holders; and it is by no means to be assumed that persons primarily rich, must therefore be just and wise,—it may not be ultimately possible so, or somewhat so, to arrange matters, as that persons primarily just and wise, should therefore be rich?

Such being the general plan of the inquiry before us, I shall not limit myself to any consecutive following of it, having hardly any good hope of being able to complete so laborious a work as it must prove to me; but from time to time, as I have leisure, shall endeavour to carry forward this part or that, as may be immediately possible; indicating always with accuracy the place which the particular essay will or should take in the completed system.

CHAPTER II.

STORE-KEEPING.

31. THE first chapter having consisted of little more than definition of terms, I purpose, in this, to expand and illustrate the given definitions.

The view which has here been taken of the nature of wealth, namely, that it consists in an intrinsic value developed by a vital power, is directly opposed to two nearly universal conceptions of wealth. In the assertion that value is primarily intrinsic, it opposes the idea that anything which is an object of desire to numbers, and is limited in quantity, so as to have rated worth in exchange, may be called, or virtually become, wealth. And in the assertion that value is, secondarily, dependent upon power in the possessor, it opposes the idea that the worth of things depends on the demand for them, instead of on the use of them. Before going farther, we will make these two positions clearer.

32. I. First. All wealth is intrinsic, and is not constituted by the judgment of men. This is easily seen in the case of things affecting the body; we know, that no force of fantasy will make stones nourishing, or poison innocent; but it is less apparent in things affecting the mind. We are easily—perhaps willingly—misled by the appearance of beneficial results obtained by industries addressed wholly to the gratification of fanciful desire; and apt to suppose that whatever is widely coveted, dearly bought, and pleasurable in possession, must be included in our definition of wealth. It is the more difficult to quit ourselves of this error because many things which are true wealth in moderate use, become false wealth in immoderate; and many things are mixed of good and evil,—as mostly, books, and works of art,—out of which one person will get the good, and another the evil; so that it seems as if there were no fixed good or evil in the things themselves, but only in the view taken, and use made of them.

But that is not so. The evil and good are fixed; in essence, and in proportion. And in things in which evil depends upon excess, the point of excess, though indefinable, is fixed; and the power of the thing is on the hither side for good, and on the farther side for evil. And in all cases this power is inherent, not dependent on opinion or choice. Our thoughts of things neither make, nor mar their eternal force; nor—which is the most serious point for future consideration—can they prevent the effect of it (within certain limits) upon ourselves.

33. Therefore, the object of any special analysis of wealth will be not so much to enumerate what is serviceable, as to distinguish what is destructive; and to show that it is inevitably destructive; that to receive pleasure from an evil thing is not to escape from, or alter the evil of it, but to be *altered by* it; that is, to suffer from it to the utmost, having our own nature, in that degree, made evil also. And it may be shown farther, that, through whatever length of time or subtleties of connexion the harm is accomplished, (being also less or more according to the

fineness and worth of the humanity on which it is wrought,) still, nothing *but* harm ever comes of a bad thing.

34. So that, in sum, the term wealth is never to be attached to the *accidental object of a morbid* desire, but only to the *constant object of a legitimate one.** By the fury of ignorance, and fitfulness of caprice, large interests may be continually attached to things unserviceable or hurtful; if their nature could be altered by our passions, the science of political Economy would remain, what it has been hitherto among us, the weighing of clouds, and the portioning out of shadows. But of ignorance there is no science; and of caprice no law. Their disturbing forces interfere with the operations of faithful Economy, but have nothing in common with them: she, the calm arbiter of national destiny, regards only essential power for good in all that she accumulates, and alike disdains the

---

* [Remember carefully this statement, that Wealth consists only in the things which the nature of humanity has rendered in all ages, and must render in all ages to come, (that is what I meant by "constant,") the objects of legitimate desire. And see Appendix II.]

wanderings* of imagination, and the thirsts of disease.

35. II. Secondly. The assertion that wealth is not *only* intrinsic, but dependent, in order to become effectual, on a given degree of vital power in its possessor, is opposed to another popular view of wealth;—namely, that though it may always be constituted by caprice, it is, when so constituted, a substantial thing, of which given quantities may be counted as existing here, or there, and exchangeable at rated prices.

In this view there are three errors. The first and chief is the overlooking the fact that all exchangeableness of commodity, or effective demand for it, depends on the sum of capacity for its use existing, here or elsewhere. The book we cannot read, or picture we take no delight in, may indeed be called part of our wealth, in so far as we have power of exchanging either for something we like better. But our power of effecting such exchange, and yet more, of effecting it to advantage, depends absolutely on the number of accessible persons who can understand the book, or enjoy the

[* The *Wanderings*, observe, not the Right goings, of Imagination. She is very far from despising these.]

painting, and who will dispute the possession of them. Thus the actual worth of either, even to us, depends no more on their essential goodness than on the capacity existing somewhere for the perception of it; and it is vain in any completed system of production to think of obtaining one without the other. So that, though the true political economist knows that co-existence of capacity for use with temporary possession cannot be always secured, the final fact, on which he bases all action and administration, is that, in the whole nation, or group of nations, he has to deal with, for every atom of intrinsic value produced he must with exactest chemistry produce its twin atom of acceptant digestion, or understanding capacity; or, in the degree of his failure, he has no wealth. Nature's challenge to us is, in earnest, as the Assyrian's mock : " I will give thee two thousand horses, if thou be able on thy part to set riders upon them." Bavieca's paces are brave, if the Cid backs him; but woe to us, if we take the dust of capacity, wearing the armour of it, for capacity itself, for so all procession, however goodly in the show of it, is to the tomb.

36. The second error in this popular view of wealth is, that in giving the name of wealth to things which we cannot use, we in reality confuse wealth with money. The land we have no skill to cultivate, the book which is sealed to us, or dress which is superfluous, may indeed be exchangeable, but as such are nothing more than a cumbrous form of banknote, of doubtful or slow convertibility. As long as we retain possession of them, we merely keep our bank-notes in the shape of gravel or clay, or book-leaves, or of embroidered tissue. Circumstances may, perhaps, render such forms the safest, or a certain complacency may attach to the exhibition of them; into both these advantages we shall inquire afterwards; I wish the reader only to observe here, that exchangeable property which we cannot use is, to us personally, merely one of the forms of money, not of wealth.

37. The third error in the popular view is the confusion of Guardianship with Possession; the real state of men of property being, too commonly, that of curators, not possessors, of wealth.

A man's power over his property is, at the

widest range of it, fivefold; it is power of Use, for himself, Administration, to others, Ostentation, Destruction, or Bequest; and possession is in use only, which for each man is sternly limited; so that such things, and so much of them as he can use, are, indeed, well for him, or Wealth; and more of them, or any other things, are ill for him, or Illth.* Plunged to the lips in Orinoco, he shall drink to his thirst measure; more at his peril: with a thousand oxen on his lands, he shall eat to his hunger measure; more, at his peril. He cannot live in two houses at once; a few bales of silk or wool will suffice for the fabric of all the clothes he can ever wear, and a few books will probably hold all the furniture good for his brain. Beyond these, in the best of us but narrow, capacities, we have but the power of administering, or *mal*-administering, wealth: (that is to say, distributing, lending, or increasing it);—of exhibiting it (as in magnificence of retinue or furniture),—of destroying, or, finally, of bequeathing it. And with multitudes of rich men, administration degenerates into curatorship; they merely hold their

* *See* Appendix III.

property in charge, as Trustees, for the benefit of some person or persons to whom it is to be delivered upon their death; and the position, explained in clear terms, would hardly seem a covetable one. What would be the probable feelings of a youth, on his entrance into life, to whom the career hoped for him was proposed in terms such as these: "You must work unremittingly, and with your utmost intelligence, during all your available years, you will thus accumulate wealth to a large amount; but you must touch none of it, beyond what is needful for your support. Whatever sums you gain, beyond those required for your decent and moderate maintenance, and whatever beautiful things you may obtain possession of, shall be properly taken care of by servants, for whose maintenance you will be charged, and whom you will have the trouble of superintending, and on your death-bed you shall have the power of determining to whom the accumulated property shall belong, or to what purposes be applied"?

38. The labour of life, under such conditions, would probably be neither zealous nor cheerful; yet the only difference between this

position and that of the ordinary capitalist is the power which the latter supposes himself to possess, and which is attributed to him by others, of spending his money at any moment. This pleasure, taken *in the imagination of power to part with that with which we have no intention of parting*, is one of the most curious, though commonest forms of the Eidolon, or Phantasm of Wealth. But the political economist has nothing to do with this idealism, and looks only to the practical issue of it—namely, that the holder of wealth, in such temper, may be regarded simply as a mechanical means of collection; or as a money-chest with a slit in it, not only receptant but suctional, set in the public thoroughfare;—chest of which only Death has the key, and evil Chance the distribution of the contents. In his function of Lender (which, however, is one of administration, not use, as far as he is himself concerned), the capitalist takes, indeed, a more interesting aspect; but even in that function, his relations with the State are apt to degenerate into a mechanism for the convenient contraction of debt;—a function the more mischievous, because a nation invariably appeases its conscience with respect to an unjustifiable expense, by meeting it with borrowed funds, expresses its repentance of a foolish piece of business, by letting its tradesmen wait for their money, and always leaves its descendants to pay for the work which will be of the least advantage to them.*

39. Quit of these three sources of misconception, the reader will have little farther difficulty in apprehending the real nature of Effectual value. He may, however, at first not without surprise, perceive the consequences involved in his acceptance of the definition. For if the actual existence of wealth be dependent on the power of its possessor, it follows that the sum of wealth held by the nation, instead of being constant or calculable, varies hourly, nay, momentarily, with the number and character of its holders! and that in changing hands, it changes in quantity. And farther, since the worth of the currency is proportioned to the sum of material

[* I would beg the reader's very close attention to these 37th and 38th paragraphs. It would be well if a dogged conviction could be enforced on nations, as on individuals, that, with few exceptions, what they cannot at present pay for, they should not at present have.]

wealth which it represents, if the sum of the wealth changes, the worth of the currency changes. And thus both the sum of the property, and power of the currency, of the State, vary momentarily as the character and number of the holders. And not only so, but different rates and kinds of variation are caused by the character of the holders of different kinds of wealth. The transitions of value caused by the character of the holders of land differ in mode from those caused by character in holders of works of art; and these again from those caused by character in holders of machinery or other working capital. But we cannot examine these special phenomena of any kind of wealth until we have a clear idea of the way in which true currency expresses them; and of the resulting modes in which the cost and price of any article are related to its value. To obtain this we must approach the subject in its first elements.

40. Let us suppose a national store of wealth, composed of material things either useful, or believed to be so, taken charge of by the Government,* and that every workman,

* See Appendix IV.

having produced any article involving labour in its production, and for which he has no immediate use, brings it to add to this store, receiving from the Government, in exchange, an order either for the return of the thing itself, or of its equivalent in other things, such as he may choose out of the store, at any time when he needs them. The question of equivalence itself (how much wine a man is to receive in return for so much corn, or how much coal in return for so much iron) is a quite separate one, which we will examine presently. For the time, let it be assumed that this equivalence has been determined, and that the Government order, in exchange for a fixed weight of any article (called, suppose, *a*), is either for the return of that weight of the article itself, or of another fixed weight of the article *b*, or another of the article *c*, and so on.

Now, supposing that the labourer speedily and continually presents these general orders, or, in common language, "spends the money," he has neither changed the circumstances of the nation, nor his own, except in so far as he may have produced useful and consumed useless articles, or *vice versâ*. But if he does not use, or uses in part only, the orders he receives, and lays aside some portion of them; and thus every day bringing his contribution to the national store, lays by some per-centage of the orders received in exchange for it, he increases the national wealth daily by as much as he does not use of the received order, and to the same amount accumulates a monetary claim on the Government. It is, of course, always in his power, as it is his legal right, to bring forward this accumulation of claim, and at once to consume, destroy, or distribute, the sum of his wealth. Supposing he never does so, but dies, leaving his claim to others, he has enriched the State during his life by the quantity of wealth over which that claim extends, or has, in other words, rendered so much additional life possible in the State, of which additional life he bequeaths the immediate possibility to those whom he invests with his claim. Supposing him to cancel the claim, he would distribute this possibility of life among the nation at large.

41. We hitherto consider the Government itself as simply a conservative power, taking charge of the wealth entrusted to it.

But a Government may be more or less than a conservative power. It may be either an improving, or destructive one.

If it be an improving power, using all the wealth entrusted to it to the best advantage, the nation is enriched in root and branch at once, and the Government is enabled, for every order presented, to return a quantity of wealth greater than the order was written for, according to the fructification obtained in the interim. This ability may be either concealed, in which case the currency does not completely represent the wealth of the country, or it may be manifested by the continual payment of the excess of value on each order, in which case there is (irrespectively, observe, of collateral results afterwards to be examined) a perpetual rise in the worth of the currency, that is to say, a fall in the price of all articles represented by it.

42. But if the Government be destructive, or a consuming power, it becomes unable to return the value received on the presentation of the order.

This inability may either be concealed by meeting demands to the full, until it issue in bankruptcy, or in some form of national debt; —or it may be concealed during oscillatory movements between destructiveness and productiveness, which result on the whole in stability;—or it may be manifested by the consistent return of less than value received on each presented order, in which case there is a consistent fall in the worth of the currency, or rise in the price of the things represented by it.

43. Now, if for this conception of a central Government, we substitute that of a body of persons occupied in industrial pursuits, of whom each adds in his private capacity to the common store, we at once obtain an approximation to the actual condition of a civilized mercantile community, from which approximation we might easily proceed into still completer analysis. I purpose, however, to arrive at every result by the gradual expansion of the simpler conception; but I wish the reader to observe, in the meantime, that both the social conditions thus supposed (and I will by anticipation say also, all possible social conditions), agree in two great points; namely, in the primal importance of the supposed

national store or stock, and in its destructibility or improveability by the holders of it.

44. I. Observe that in both conditions, that of central Government-holding, and diffused private-holding, the quantity of stock is of the same national moment. In the one case, indeed, its amount may be known by examination of the persons to whom it is confided; in the other it cannot be known but by exposing the private affairs of every individual. But, known or unknown, its significance is the same under each condition. The riches of the nation consist in the abundance, and their wealth depends on the nature, of this store.

45. II. In the second place, both conditions (and all other possible ones) agree in the destructibility or improveability of the store by its holders. Whether in private hands, or under Government charge, the national store may be daily consumed, or daily enlarged, by its possessors; and while the currency remains apparently unaltered, the property it represents may diminish or increase.

46. The first question, then, which we have to put under our simple conception of central Government, namely, "What store has it?"

is one of equal importance, whatever may be the constitution of the State; while the second question—namely, "Who are the holders of the store?" involves the discussion of the constitution of the State itself.

The first inquiry resolves itself into three heads:

1. What is the nature of the store?
2. What is its quantity in relation to the population?
3. What is its quantity in relation to the currency?

The second inquiry into two:

1. Who are the Holders of the store, and in what proportions?
2. Who are the Claimants of the store (that is to say, the holders of the currency), and in what proportions?

We will examine the range of the first three questions in the present paper; of the two following, in the sequel.

47. I. QUESTION FIRST. What is the nature of the store? Has the nation hitherto worked for and gathered the right thing or the wrong? On that issue rest the possibilities of its life.

For example, let us imagine a society, of no

great extent, occupied in procuring and laying up store of corn, wine, wool, silk, and other such preservable materials of food and clothing; and that it has a currency representing them. Imagine farther, that on days of festivity, the society, discovering itself to derive satisfaction from pyrotechnics, gradually turns its attention more and more to the manufacture of gunpowder; so that an increasing number of labourers, giving what time they can spare to this branch of industry, bring increasing quantities of combustibles into the store, and use the general orders received in exchange to obtain such wine, wool, or corn, as they may have need of. The currency remains the same, and represents precisely the same amount of material in the store, and of labour spent in producing it. But the corn and wine gradually vanish, and in their place, as gradually, appear sulphur and saltpetre, till at last the labourers who have consumed corn and supplied nitre, presenting on a festal morning some of their currency to obtain materials for the feast, discover that no amount of currency will command anything Festive, except Fire. The supply of rockets is unlimited, but that of food, limited, in a quite final manner; and the whole currency in the hands of the society represents an infinite power of detonation, but none of existence.

48. This statement, caricatured as it may seem, is only exaggerated in assuming the persistence of the folly to extremity, unchecked, as in reality it would be, by the gradual rise in price of food. But it falls short of the actual facts of human life in expression of the depth and intensity of the folly itself. For a great part (the reader would not believe how great until he saw the statistics in detail) of the most earnest and ingenious industry of the world is spent in producing munitions of war; gathering, that is to say, the materials, not of festive, but of consuming fire; filling its stores with all power of the instruments of pain, and all affluence of the ministries of death. It was no true *Trionfo della Morte** which men have seen and feared (sometimes scarcely feared) so long; wherein he brought them rest from

[* I little thought, what *Trionfo della Morte* would be, for this very cause, and in literal fulfilment of the closing words of the 47th paragraph, over the fields and houses of Europe, and over its fairest city—within seven years from the day I wrote it.]

their labours. We see, and share, another and higher form of his triumph now. Taskmaster, instead of Releaser, he rules the dust of the arena no less than of the tomb; and, content once in the grave whither man went, to make his works to cease and his devices to vanish,—now, in the busy city and on the serviceable sea, makes his work to increase, and his devices to multiply.

49. To this doubled loss, or negative power of labour, spent in producing means of destruction, we have to add, in our estimate of the consequences of human folly, whatever more insidious waste of toil there is in production of unnecessary luxury. Such and such an occupation (it is said) supports so many labourers, because so many obtain wages in following it; but it is never considered that unless there be a supporting power in the product of the occupation, the wages given to one man are merely withdrawn from another. We cannot say of any trade that it maintains such and such a number of persons, unless we know how and where the money, now spent in the purchase of its produce, would have been spent, if that produce had not been

manufactured. The purchasing funds truly support a number of people in making This; but (probably) leave unsupported an equal number who are making, or could have made That. The manufacturers of small watches thrive at Geneva;—it is well;—but where would the money spent on small watches have gone, had there been no small watches to buy?

50. If the so frequently uttered aphorism of mercantile economy—" Labour is limited by capital," were true, this question would be a definite one. But it is untrue; and that widely. Out of a given quantity of funds for wages, more or less labour is to be had, according to the quantity of will with which we can inspire the workman; and the true limit of labour is only in the limit of this moral stimulus of the will, and of the bodily power. In an ultimate, but entirely unpractical sense, labour is limited by capital, as it is by matter—that is to say, where there is no material, there can be no work,—but in the practical sense, labour is limited only by the great original capital of head, heart, and hand. Even in the most artificial relations

of commerce, labour is to capital as fire to fuel: out of so much fuel, you *can* have only so much fire; but out of so much fuel you *shall* have so much fire,—not in proportion to the mass of combustible, but to the force of wind that fans and water that quenches; and the appliance of both. And labour is furthered, as conflagration is, not so much by added fuel, as by admitted air.*

51. For which reasons, I had to insert, in § 49, the qualifying "probably;" for it can never be said positively that the purchase-money, or wages fund of any trade is withdrawn from some other trade. The object itself may be the stimulus of the production of the money which buys it; that is to say, the work by which the purchaser obtained the means of buying it, would not have been done by him, unless he had wanted that particular thing. And the production of any article not intrinsically (nor in the process of manufacture)

[* The meaning of which is, that you may spend a great deal of money, and get very little work for it, and that little bad; but having good "air," or "spirit," to put life into it, with very little money, you may get a great deal of work, and all good; which, observe, is an arithmetical, not at all a poetical or visionary circumstance.]

injurious, is useful, if the desire of it causes productive labour in other directions.

52. In the national store, therefore, the presence of things intrinsically valueless does not imply an entirely correlative absence of things valuable. We cannot be certain that all the labour spent on vanity has been diverted from reality, and that for every bad thing produced, a precious thing has been lost. In great measure, the vain things represent the results of roused indolence; they have been carved, as toys, in extra time; and, if they had not been made, nothing else would have been made. Even to munitions of war this principle applies; they partly represent the work of men who, if they had not made spears, would never have made pruning-hooks, and who are incapable of any activities but those of contest.

53. Thus then, finally, the nature of the store has to be considered under two main lights; the one, that of its immediate and actual utility; the other, that of the past national character which it signifies by its production, and future character which it must develope by its use. And the issue of this investigation will be to show us that

Economy does not depend merely on principles of "demand and supply," but primarily on what is demanded, and what is supplied; which I will beg of you to observe, and take to heart.

54. II. QUESTION SECOND.—What is the quantity of the store in relation to the population?

It follows from what has been already stated that the accurate form in which this question has to be put is—"What quantity of each article composing the store exists in proportion to the real need for it by the population?" But we shall for the time assume, in order to keep all our terms at the simplest, that the store is wholly composed of useful articles, and accurately proportioned to the several needs for them.

Now it cannot be assumed, because the store is large in proportion to the number of the people, that the people must be in comfort; nor because it is small, that they must be in distress. An active and economical race always produces more than it requires, and lives (if it is permitted to do so) in competence on the produce of its daily labour. The quantity of its store, great or small, is therefore in many respects indifferent to it, and cannot be inferred from its aspect. Similarly an inactive and wasteful population, which cannot live by its daily labour, but is dependent, partly or wholly, on consumption of its store, may be (by various difficulties, hereafter to be examined, in realizing or getting at such store) retained in a state of abject distress, though its possessions may be immense. But the results always involved in the magnitude of store are, the commercial power of the nation, its security, and its mental character. Its commercial power, in that according to the quantity of its store may be the extent of its dealings; its security, in that according to the quantity of its store are its means of sudden exertion or sustained endurance; and its character, in that certain conditions of civilization cannot be attained without permanent and continually accumulating store, of great intrinsic value, and of peculiar nature.*

55. Now, seeing that these three advantages arise from largeness of store in proportion to

[* More especially, works of great art.]

population, the question arises immediately, "Given the store—is the nation enriched by diminution of its numbers? Are a successful national speculation, and a pestilence, economically the same thing?"

This is in part a sophistical question; such as it would be to ask whether a man was richer when struck by disease which must limit his life within a predicable period, than he was when in health. He is enabled to enlarge his current expenses, and has for all purposes a larger sum at his immediate disposal (for, given the fortune, the shorter the life, the larger the annuity); yet no man considers himself richer because he is condemned by his physician.

56. The logical reply is that, since Wealth is by definition only the means of life, a nation cannot be enriched by its own mortality. Or in shorter words, the life is more than the meat; and existence itself, more wealth than the means of existence. Whence, of two nations who have equal store, the more numerous is to be considered the richer, provided the type of the inhabitant be as high (for, though the relative bulk of their store

be less, its relative efficiency, or the amount of effectual wealth, must be greater). But if the type of the population be deteriorated by increase of its numbers, we have evidence of poverty in its worst influence; and then, to determine whether the nation in its total may still be justifiably esteemed rich, we must set or weigh, the number of the poor against that of the rich.

To effect which piece of scale-work, it is of course necessary to determine, first, who are poor and who are rich; nor this only, but also how poor and how rich they are. Which will prove a curious thermometrical investigation; for we shall have to do for gold and for silver, what we have done for quicksilver;—determine, namely, their freezing-point, their zero, their temperate and fever-heat points; finally, their vaporescent point, at which riches, sometimes explosively, as lately in America, "make to themselves wings:"— and correspondently, the number of degrees *below* zero at which poverty, ceasing to brace with any wholesome cold, burns to the bone.*

[* The meaning of that, in plain English, is, that we must find out how far poverty and riches are good or bad

II.—STORE-KEEPING.

57. For the performance of these operations, in the strictest sense scientific, we will first look to the existing so-called "science" of Political Economy; we will ask it to define for us the comparatively and superlatively rich, and the comparatively and superlatively poor; and on its own terms—if any terms it can pronounce—examine, in our prosperous England, how many rich and how many poor people there are; and whether the quantity and intensity of the poverty is indeed so overbalanced by the quantity and intensity of wealth, that we may permit ourselves a luxurious blindness to it, and call ourselves, complacently, a rich country. And if we find no clear definition in the existing science, we will endeavour for ourselves to fix the true degrees of the scale, and to apply them.*

for people, and what is the difference between being miserably poor—so as, perhaps, to be driven to crime, or to pass life in suffering—and being blessedly poor, in the sense meant in the Sermon on the Mount. For I suppose the people who believe that sermon, do not think (if they ever honestly ask themselves what they do think), either that Luke vi. 24 is a merely poetical exclamation, or that the Beatitude of Poverty has yet been attained in St. Martin's Lane and other back streets of London.]

[* Large plans!—Eight years are gone, and nothing

58. III. QUESTION THIRD. What is the quantity of the store in relation to the Currency?

We have seen that the real worth of the currency, so far as dependent on its relation to the magnitude of the store, may vary, within certain limits, without affecting its worth in exchange. The diminution or increase of the represented wealth may be unperceived, and the currency may be taken either for more or less than it is truly worth. Usually it is taken for much more; and its power in exchange, or credit-power, is thus increased up to a given strain upon its relation to existing wealth. This credit-power is of chief importance in the thoughts, because most sharply present to the experience, of a mercantile community: but the conditions of its stability* and all other relations of the currency

done yet. But I keep my purpose of making one day this balance, or want of balance, visible, in those so seldom used scales of Justice.]

* These are nearly all briefly represented by the image used for the force of money by Dante, of mast and sail:—

>Quali dal vento le gonfiate vele
>Caggiono avvolte, poi chè l'alber fiacca
>Tal cadde a terra la fiera crudele.

The image may be followed out, like all of Dante's, into

to the material store are entirely simple in principle, if not in action. Far other than simple are the relations of the currency to the available labour which it also represents. For this relation is involved not only with that of the magnitude of the store to the number, but with that of the magnitude of the store to the mind, of the population. Its proportion to their number, and the resulting worth of currency, are calculable; but its proportion to their will for labour is not. The worth of the piece of money which claims a given quantity of the store is, in exchange, less or greater according to the facility of obtaining the same quantity of the same thing without having recourse to the store. In other words, it

as close detail as the reader chooses. Thus the stress of the sail must be proportioned to the strength of the mast, and it is only in unforeseen danger that a skilful seaman ever carries all the canvas his spars will bear; states of mercantile languor are like the flap of the sail in a calm; of mercantile precaution, like taking in reefs; and mercantile ruin is instant on the breaking of the mast.

[I mean by credit-power, the general impression on the national mind that a sovereign, or any other coin, is worth so much bread and cheese—so much wine—so much horse and carriage—or so much fine art: it may be really worth, when tried, less or more than is thought: the thought of it is the credit-power.]

depends on the immediate Cost and Price of the thing. We must now, therefore, complete the definition of these terms.

59. All cost and price are counted in Labour. We must know first, therefore, what is to be counted *as* Labour.

I have already defined Labour to be the Contest of the life of man with an opposite. Literally, it is the quantity of "Lapse," loss, or failure of human life, caused by any effort. It is usually confused with effort itself, or the application of power (opera); but there is much effort which is merely a mode of re-creation, or of pleasure. The most beautiful actions of the human body, and the highest results of the human intelligence, are conditions, or achievements, of quite unlaborious, —nay, of recreative,—effort. But labour is the *suffering* in effort. It is the negative quantity, or quantity of de-feat, which has to be counted against every Feat, and of de-fect, which has to be counted against every Fact, or Deed of men. In brief, it is "that quantity of our toil which we die in."

We might, therefore, *à priori*, conjecture (as we shall ultimately find), that it cannot be bought, nor sold. Everything else is bought and sold for Labour, but Labour itself cannot be bought nor sold for anything, being priceless.* The idea that it is a commodity to be bought or sold, is the alpha and omega of Politico-Economic fallacy.

60. This being the nature of labour, the "Cost" of anything is the quantity of labour necessary to obtain it;—the quantity for which, or at which, it "stands" (constat). It is literally the "Constancy" of the thing;—you shall win it—move it—come at it, for no less than this.

Cost is measured and measurable (using the accurate Latin terms) only in "labor," not in "opera."† It does not matter how much *work*

---

* The object of Political Economy is not to buy, nor to sell labour, but to spare it. Every attempt to buy or sell it is, in the outcome, ineffectual; so far as successful, it is not sale, but Betrayal; and the purchase-money is a part of that thirty pieces which bought, first the greatest of labours, and afterwards the burial-field of the Stranger; for this purchase-money, being in its very smallness or vileness the exactly measured opposite of the "vilis annona amicorum," makes all men strangers to each other.

† Cicero's distinction, "sordidi quæstus, quorum operæ, non quorum artes emuntur," admirable in principle, is inaccurate in expression, because Cicero did not practically

a thing needs to produce it; it matters only how much *distress*. Generally the more the power it requires, the less the distress; so that the noblest works of man cost less than the meanest.

True labour, or spending of life, is either of the body, in fatigue or pain; of the temper or heart (as in perseverance of search for things,—patience in waiting for them,—fortitude or degradation in suffering for them, and the like), or of the intellect. All these kinds of labour are supposed to be included in the general term, and the quantity of labour is then expressed by the time it lasts. So that a unit of labour is "an hour's work" or a day's work, as we may determine.*

61. Cost, like value, is both intrinsic and

---

know how much operative dexterity is necessary in all the higher arts; but the cost of this dexterity is incalculable. Be it great or small, the "cost" of the mere perfectness of touch in a hammer-stroke of Donatello's, or a pencil-touch of Correggio's, is inestimable by any ordinary arithmetic.

[Old notes, these, more embarrassing, I now perceive, than elucidatory; but right, and worth retaining.]

* Only observe, as some labour is more destructive of life than other labour, the hour or day of the more destructive toil is supposed to include proportionate rest. Though men do not, or cannot, usually take such rest, except in death.

effectual. Intrinsic cost is that of getting the thing in the right way; effectual cost is that of getting the thing in the way we set about it. But intrinsic cost cannot be made a subject of analytical investigation, being only partially discoverable, and that by long experience. Effectual cost is all that the political economist can deal with; that is to say, the cost of the thing under existing circumstances, and by known processes.

Cost, being dependent much on application of method, varies with the quantity of the thing wanted, and with the number of persons who work for it. It is easy to get a little of some things, but difficult to get much; it is impossible to get some things with few hands, but easy to get them with many.

62. The cost and value of things, however difficult to determine accurately, are thus both dependent on ascertainable physical circumstances.*

* There is, therefore, observe, no such thing as cheapness (in the common use of that term), without some error or injustice. A thing is said to be cheap, not because it is common, but because it is supposed to be sold under its worth. Everything has its proper and true worth at any given time, in relation to everything else; and at that worth

But their *price* is dependent on the human will.

Such and such a thing is demonstrably good for so much. And it may demonstrably be had for so much.

should be bought and sold. If sold under it, it is cheap to the buyer by exactly so much as the seller loses, and no more. Putrid meat, at twopence a pound, is not "cheaper" than wholesome meat at sevenpence a pound; it is probably much dearer; but if, by watching your opportunity, you can get the wholesome meat for sixpence a pound, it is cheaper to you by a penny, which you have gained, and the seller has lost. The present rage for cheapness is either, therefore, simply and literally a rage for badness of all commodities, or it is an attempt to find persons whose necessities will force them to let you have more than you should for your money. It is quite easy to produce such persons, and in large numbers; for the more distress there is in a nation, the more cheapness of this sort you can obtain, and your boasted cheapness is thus merely a measure of the extent of your national distress.

There is, indeed, a condition of apparent cheapness, which we have some right to be triumphant in; namely, the real reduction in cost of articles by right application of labour. But in this case the article is only cheap with reference to its *former* price; the so-called cheapness is only our expression for the sensation of contrast between its former and existing prices. So soon as the new methods of producing the article are established, it ceases to be esteemed either cheap or dear, at the new price, as at the old one, and is felt to be cheap only when accident enables it to be purchased beneath this new value. And it is no advantage to produce the article more easily, except as it enables you to multiply your

II.—STORE-KEEPING.

But it remains questionable, and in all manner of ways questionable, whether I choose to give so much.*

This choice is always a relative one. It is a choice to give a price for this, rather than for

population. Cheapness of this kind is merely the discovery that more men can be maintained on the same ground; and the question how many you will maintain in proportion to your additional means, remains exactly in the same terms that it did before.

A form of immediate cheapness results, however, in many cases, without distress, from the labour of a population where food is redundant, or where the labour by which the food is produced leaves much idle time on their hands, which may be applied to the production of "cheap" articles.

All such phenomena indicate to the political economist places where the labour is unbalanced. In the first case, the just balance is to be effected by taking labourers from the spot where pressure exists, and sending them to that where food is redundant. In the second, the cheapness is a local accident, advantageous to the local purchaser, disadvantageous to the local producer. It is one of the first duties of commerce to extend the market, and thus give the local producer his full advantage.

Cheapness caused by natural accidents of harvest, weather, etc., is always counterbalanced, in due time, by natural scarcity, similarly caused. It is the part of wise government, and healthy commerce, so to provide in times and places of plenty for times and places of dearth, as that there shall never be waste, nor famine.

Cheapness caused by gluts of the market is merely a disease of clumsy and wanton commerce.

* Price has been already defined (p. 10) to be the quantity

that;—a resolution to have the thing, if getting it does not involve the loss of a better thing. Price depends, therefore, not only on the cost of the commodity itself, but on its relation to the cost of every other attainable thing.

Farther. The *power* of choice is also a relative one. It depends not merely on our own estimate of the thing, but on everybody else's estimate; therefore on the number and force of the will of the concurrent buyers, and on the existing quantity of the thing in proportion to that number and force.

Hence the price of anything depends on four variables.

(1.) Its cost.

(2.) Its attainable quantity at that cost.

(3.) The number and power of the persons who want it.

(4.) The estimate they have formed of its desirableness.

Its value only affects its price so far as it is

of labour which the possessor of a thing is willing to take for it. It is best to consider the price to be that fixed by the possessor, because the possessor has absolute power of refusing sale, while the purchaser has no absolute power of compelling it; but the effectual or market price is that at which their estimates coincide.

II.—STORE-KEEPING.

contemplated in this estimate; perhaps, therefore, not at all.

63. Now, in order to show the manner in which price is expressed in terms of a currency, we must assume these four quantities to be known, and "the estimate of desirableness," commonly called the Demand, to be certain. We will take the number of persons at the lowest. Let A and B be two labourers who "demand," that is to say, have resolved to labour for, two articles, a and b. Their demand for these articles (if the reader likes better, he may say their need) is to be conceived as absolute, their existence depending on the getting these two things. Suppose, for instance, that they are bread and fuel, in a cold country, and let a represent the least quantity of bread, and b the least quantity of fuel, which will support a man's life for a day. Let a be producible by an hour's labour, but b only by two hours' labour.

Then the *cost* of a is one hour, and of b two (cost, by our definition, being expressible in terms of time). If, therefore, each man worked both for his corn and fuel, each would have to work three hours a day. But they divide the labour for its greater ease.* Then if A works three hours, he produces 3 a, which is one a more than both the men want. And if B works three hours, he produces only $1\frac{1}{2}$ b, or half of b less than both want. But if A work three hours and B six, A has 3 a, and B has 3 b, a maintenance in the right proportion for both for a day and a half; so that each might take half a day's rest. But as B has worked double time, the whole of this day's rest belongs in equity to him. Therefore the just exchange should be, A giving two a for one b, has one a and one b;—maintenance for a day. B giving one b for two a, has two a and two b;—maintenance for two days.

But B cannot rest on the second day, or A would be left without the article which B produces. Nor is there any means of making the exchange just, unless a third labourer is called in. Then one workman, A, produces a, and two, B and C, produce b:—A, working three hours, has three a;—B, three hours, $1\frac{1}{2}$ b;—

---

* This "greater ease" ought to be allowed for by a diminution in the times of the divided work; but as the proportion of times would remain the same, I do not introduce this unnecessary complexity into the calculation.

C, three hours, 1½ *b*. B and C each give half of *b* for *a*, and all have their equal daily maintenance for equal daily work.

To carry the example a single step farther, let three articles, *a*, *b*, and *c* be needed.

Let *a* need one hour's work, *b* two, and *c* four; then the day's work must be seven hours, and one man in a day's work can make 7 *a*, or 3½ *b*, or 1¾ *c*.

Therefore one A works for *a*, producing 7 *a*; two B's work for *b*, producing 7 *b*; four C's work for *c*, producing 7 *c*.

A has six *a* to spare, and gives two *a* for one *b*, and four *a* for one *c*. Each B has 2½ *b* to spare, and gives ½ *b* for one *a*, and two *b* for one *c*.

Each C has ¾ of *c* to spare, and gives ½ *c* for one *b*, and ¼ of *c* for one *a*.

And all have their day's maintenance.

Generally, therefore, it follows that if the demand is constant,* the relative prices of things are as their costs, or as the quantities of labour involved in production.

64. Then, in order to express their prices in terms of a currency, we have only to put the

---

* Compare *Unto this Last*, p. 115, *et seq.*

currency into the form of orders for a certain quantity of any given article (with us it is in the form of orders for gold), and all quantities of other articles are priced by the relation they bear to the article which the currency claims.

But the worth of the currency itself is not in the slightest degree founded more on the worth of the article which it either claims or consists in (as gold) than on the worth of every other article for which the gold is exchangeable. It is just as accurate to say, "so many pounds are worth an acre of land," as "an acre of land is worth so many pounds." The worth of gold, of land, of houses, and of food, and of all other things, depends at any moment on the existing quantities and relative demands for all and each; and a change in the worth of, or demand for, any one, involves an instantaneously correspondent change in the worth of, and demand for, all the rest;—a change as inevitable and as accurately balanced (though often in its process as untraceable) as the change in volume of the outflowing river from some vast lake, caused by change in the volume of the inflowing streams, though no eye can trace, nor instrument detect, motion, either on its surface, or in the depth.

65. Thus, then, the real working power or worth of the currency is founded on the entire sum of the relative estimates formed by the population of its possessions; a change in this estimate in any direction (and therefore every change in the national character), instantly alters the value of money, in its second great function of commanding labour. But we must always carefully and sternly distinguish between this worth of currency, dependent on the conceived or appreciated value of what it represents, and the worth of it, dependent on the *existence* of what it represents. A currency is *true or false*, in proportion to the security with which it gives claim to the possession of land, house, horse, or picture; but a currency is *strong or weak*,* worth much or worth little, in proportion to the degree of estimate in which the nation holds the house, horse, or picture which is claimed. Thus the power of

[* That is to say, the love of money is founded first on the intenseness of desire for given things; a youth will rob the till, now-a-days, for pantomime tickets and cigars; the "strength" of the currency being irresistible to him, in consequence of his desire for those luxuries.]

the English currency has been, till of late, largely based on the national estimate of horses and of wine: so that a man might always give any price to furnish choicely his stable, or his cellar; and receive public approval therefore: but if he gave the same sum to furnish his library, he was called mad, or a biblio-maniac. And although he might lose his fortune by his horses, and his health or life by his cellar, and rarely lost either by his books, he was yet never called a Hippomaniac nor an Oino-maniac; but only Bibliomaniac, because the current worth of money was understood to be legitimately founded on cattle and wine, but not on literature. The prices lately given at sales for pictures and MSS. indicate some tendency to change in the national character in this respect, so that the worth of the currency may even come in time to rest, in an acknowledged manner, somewhat on the state and keeping of the Bedford missal, as well as on the health of Caractacus or Blink Bonny; and old pictures be considered property, no less than old port. They might have been so before now, but that it is more difficult to choose the one than the other.

66. Now, observe, all these sources of variation in the power of the currency exist, wholly irrespective of the influences of vice, indolence, and improvidence. We have hitherto supposed, throughout the analysis, every professing labourer to labour honestly, heartily, and in harmony with his fellows. We have now to bring farther into the calculation the effects of relative industry, honour, and forethought; and thus to follow out the bearings of our second inquiry: Who are the holders of the Store and Currency, and in what proportions?

This, however, we must reserve for our next paper—noticing here only that, however distinct the several branches of the subject are, radically, they are so interwoven in their issues that we cannot rightly treat any one, till we have taken cognizance of all. Thus the need of the currency in proportion to number of population is materially influenced by the probable number of the holders in proportion to the non-holders; and this again, by the number of holders of goods, or wealth, in proportion to the non-holders of goods. For as, by definition, the currency is a claim to goods which are not possessed, its quantity indicates the number of claimants in proportion to the number of holders; and the force and complexity of claim. For if the claims be not complex, currency as a means of exchange may be very small in quantity. A sells some corn to B, receiving a promise from B to pay in cattle, which A then hands over to C, to get some wine. C in due time claims the cattle from B; and B takes back his promise. These exchanges have, or might have been, all effected with a single coin or promise; and the proportion of the currency to the store would in such circumstances indicate only the circulating vitality of it—that is to say, the quantity and convenient divisibility of that part of the store which the *habits* of the nation keep in circulation. If a cattle breeder is content to live with his household chiefly on meat and milk, and does not want rich furniture, or jewels, or books—if a wine and corn grower maintains himself and his men chiefly on grapes and bread;—if the wives and daughters of families weave and spin the clothing of the household, and the nation, as a whole, remains content with the produce of its own soil and the work of its own hands, it has little occasion for circulating media. It pledges and promises little and seldom; exchanges only so far as exchange is necessary for life. The store belongs to the people in whose hands it is found, and money is little needed either as an expression of right, or practical means of division and exchange.

67. But in proportion as the habits of the nation become complex and fantastic (and they may be both, without therefore being civilized), its circulating medium must increase in proportion to its store. If every one wants a little of everything,—if food must be of many kinds, and dress of many fashions,—if multitudes live by work which, ministering to fancy, has its pay measured by fancy, so that large prices will be given by one person for what is valueless to another,—if there are great inequalities of knowledge, causing great inequalities of estimate,—and, finally, and worst of all, if the currency itself, from its largeness, and the power which the possession of it implies, becomes the sole object of desire with large numbers of the nation, so that the holding of it is disputed among them as the

main object of life:—in each and all of these cases, the currency necessarily enlarges in proportion to the store; and as a means of exchange and division, as a bond of right, and as an object of passion, has a more and more important and malignant power over the nation's dealings, character, and life.

Against which power, when, as a bond of Right, it becomes too conspicuous and too burdensome, the popular voice is apt to be raised in a violent and irrational manner, leading to revolution instead of remedy. Whereas all possibility of Economy depends on the clear assertion and maintenance of this bond of right, however burdensome. The first necessity of all economical government is to secure the unquestioned and unquestionable working of the great law of Property—that a man who works for a thing shall be allowed to get it, keep it, and consume it, in peace; and that he who does not eat his cake to-day, shall be seen, without grudging, to have his cake to-morrow. This, I say, is the first point to be secured by social law; without this, no political advance, nay, no political existence, is in any sort possible. Whatever evil, luxury, iniquity, may seem to result from it, this is nevertheless the first of all Equities; and to the enforcement of this, by law and police-truncheon, the nation must always primarily set its mind—that the cupboard door may have a firm lock to it, and no man's dinner be carried off by the mob, on its way home from the baker's. Which, thus fearlessly asserting, we shall endeavour in next paper to consider how far it may be practicable for the mob itself, also, in due breadth of dish, to have dinners to carry home.

CHAPTER III.

COIN-KEEPING.

68. IT will be seen by reference to the last chapter that our present task is to examine the relation of holders of store to holders of currency; and of both to those who hold neither. In order to do this, we must determine on which side we are to place substances such as gold, commonly known as bases of currency. By aid of previous definitions the reader will now be able to understand closer statements than have yet been possible.

69. *The currency of any country consists of every document acknowledging debt, which is transferable in the country.**

This transferableness depends upon its intelligibility and credit. Its intelligibility

[* Remember this definition : it is of great importance as opposed to the imperfect ones usually given. When first these essays were published, I remember one of their

III.—COIN-KEEPING.

depends chiefly on the difficulty of forging anything like it ;—its credit much on national character, but ultimately *always on the existence of substantial means of meeting its demand.**

As the degrees of transferableness are variable, (some documents passing only in certain places, and others passing, if at all, for less than their inscribed value,) both the mass, and, so to speak, fluidity, of the currency, are variable. True or perfect currency flows freely, like a pure stream; it becomes sluggish or stagnant in proportion to the quantity of less transferable matter which mixes with it, adding to its bulk, but diminishing its purity. [Articles of commercial value, on which bills are drawn, increase the currency indefinitely; and substances of intrinsic value, if stamped or signed without restriction so as to become acknowledgments of debt, increase it indefinitely also.] Every

reviewers asking contemptuously, " Is half-a-crown a document?" it never having before occurred to him that a document might be stamped as well as written, and stamped on silver as well as on parchment.]

[* I do not mean the demand of the holder of a five-pound note for five pounds, but the demand of the holder of a pound for a pound's worth of something good.]

bit of gold found in Australia, so long as it remains uncoined, is an article offered for sale like any other; but as soon as it is coined into pounds, it diminishes the value of every pound we have now in our pockets.

70. Legally authorized or national currency, in its perfect condition, is a form of public acknowledgment of debt, so regulated and divided that any person presenting a commodity of tried worth in the public market, shall, if he please, receive in exchange for it a document giving him claim to the return of its equivalent, (1) in any place, (2) at any time, and (3) in any kind.

When currency is quite healthy and vital, the persons entrusted with its management are always able to give on demand either,

A. The assigning document for the assigned quantity of goods. Or,

B. The assigned quantity of goods for the assigning document.

If they cannot give document for goods, the national exchange is at fault.

If they cannot give goods for document, the national credit is at fault.

The nature and power of the document are

therefore to be examined under the three relations it bears to Place, Time, and Kind.

71. (1.) It gives claim to the return of equivalent wealth in any *Place*. Its use in this function is to save carriage, so that parting with a bushel of corn in London, we may receive an order for a bushel of corn at the Antipodes, or elsewhere. To be perfect in this use, the substance of currency must be to the maximum portable, credible, and intelligible. Its non-acceptance or discredit results always from some form of ignorance or dishonour: so far as such interruptions rise out of differences in denomination, there is no ground for their continuance among civilized nations. It may be convenient in one country to use chiefly copper for coinage, in another silver, and in another gold,—reckoning accordingly in centimes, francs, or zecchins: but that a franc should be different in weight and value from a shilling, and a zwanziger vary from both, is wanton loss of commercial power.

72. (2.) It gives claim to the return of equivalent wealth at any *Time*. In this second use, currency is the exponent of accumulation:

it renders the laying-up of store at the command of individuals unlimitedly possible;—whereas, but for its intervention, all gathering would be confined within certain limits by the bulk of property, or by its decay, or the difficulty of its guardianship. "I will pull down my barns and build greater," cannot be a daily saying; and all material investment is enlargement of care. The national currency transfers the guardianship of the store to many; and preserves to the original producer the right of re-entering on its possession at any future period.

73. (3.) It gives claim (practical, though not legal) to the return of equivalent wealth in any *Kind*. It is a transferable right, not merely to this or that, but to anything; and its power in this function is proportioned to the range of choice. If you give a child an apple or a toy, you give him a determinate pleasure, but if you give him a penny, an indeterminate one, proportioned to the range of selection offered by the shops in the village. The power of the world's currency is similarly in proportion to the openness of the world's fair, and, commonly, enhanced by the brilliancy

of external aspect, rather than solidity, of its wares.

74. We have said that the currency consists of orders for equivalent goods. If equivalent, their quality must be guaranteed. The kinds of goods chosen for specific claim must, therefore, be capable of test, while, also, that a store may be kept in hand to meet the call of the currency, smallness of bulk, with great relative value, is desirable; and indestructibility, over at least a certain period, essential.

Such indestructibility, and facility of being tested, are united in gold; its intrinsic value is great, and its imaginary value greater; so that, partly through indolence, partly through necessity and want of organization, most nations have agreed to take gold for the only basis of their currencies;—with this grave disadvantage, that its portability enabling the metal to become an active part of the medium of exchange, the stream of the currency itself becomes opaque with gold—half currency and half commodity, in unison of functions which partly neutralize, partly enhance, each other's force.

75. They partly neutralize, since in so far as the gold is commodity, it is bad currency, because liable to sale; and in so far as it is currency, it is bad commodity, because its exchange value interferes with its practical use. Especially its employment in the higher branches of the arts becomes unsafe on account of its liability to be melted down for exchange.

Again. They partly enhance, since in so far as the gold has acknowledged intrinsic value, it is good currency, because everywhere acceptable; and in so far as it has legal exchangeable value, its worth as a commodity is increased. We want no gold in the form of dust or crystal; but we seek for it coined, because in that form it will pay baker and butcher. And this worth in exchange not only absorbs a large quantity in that use,*

---

* [Read and think over, the following note very carefully.]

The waste of labour in obtaining the gold, though it cannot be estimated by help of any existing data, may be understood in its bearing on entire economy by supposing it limited to transactions between two persons. If two farmers in Australia have been exchanging corn and cattle with each other for years, keeping their accounts of reciprocal debt in any simple way, the sum of the possessions of either would not be diminished, though the part of it which was lent or

but greatly increases the effect on the imagination of the quantity used in the arts. Thus, in brief, the force of the functions is increased, but their precision blunted, by their unison.

76. These inconveniences, however, attach to gold as a basis of currency on account of its portability and preciousness. But a far greater inconvenience attaches to it as the only legal basis of currency. Imagine gold to be only attainable in masses weighing several pounds each, and its value, like that of malachite or marble, proportioned to its largeness of bulk;—it could not then get itself confused with the currency in daily use, but it might still remain as its basis; and this second inconvenience would still affect it, namely, that its significance as an expression of debt varies, as that of every other article would, with the popular estimate of its desirableness,

borrowed were only reckoned by marks on a stone, or notches on a tree; and the one counted himself accordingly, so many scratches, or so many notches, better than the other. But it would soon be seriously diminished if, discovering gold in their fields, each resolved only to accept golden counters for a reckoning; and accordingly, whenever he wanted a sack of corn or a cow, was obliged to go and wash sand for a week before he could get the means of giving a receipt for them.

and with the quantity offered in the market. My power of obtaining other goods for gold depends always on the strength of public passion for gold, and on the limitation of its quantity, so that when either of two things happens—that the world esteems gold less, or finds it more easily—*my right of claim is in that degree effaced;* and it has been even gravely maintained that a discovery of a mountain of gold would cancel the National Debt; in other words, that men may be paid for what costs much in what costs nothing. Now, it is true that there is little chance of sudden convulsion in this respect; the world will not so rapidly increase in wisdom as to despise gold on a sudden; and perhaps may [for a little time] desire it more eagerly the more easily it is obtained; nevertheless, the right of debt ought not to rest on a basis of imagination; nor should the frame of a national currency vibrate with every miser's panic, and every merchant's imprudence.

77. There are two methods of avoiding this insecurity, which would have been fallen upon long ago, if, instead of calculating the conditions of the supply of gold, men had only

considered how the world might live and manage its affairs without gold at all.* One is, to base the currency on substances of truer intrinsic value; the other, to base it on several substances instead of one. If I can only claim gold, the discovery of a golden mountain starves me; but if I can claim bread, the discovery of a continent of corn-fields need not trouble me. If, however, I wish to exchange my bread for other things, a good harvest will for the time limit my power in this respect; but if I can claim either bread, iron, or silk at pleasure, the standard of value has three feet instead of one, and will be proportionately firm. Thus, ultimately, the steadiness of currency depends upon the breadth of its base; but the difficulty of organization increasing with this breadth, the discovery of

---

* It is difficult to estimate the curious futility of discussions such as that which lately occupied a section of the British Association, on the absorption of gold, while no one can produce even the simplest of the data necessary for the inquiry. To take the first occurring one,—What means have we of ascertaining the weight of gold employed this year in the toilettes of the women of Europe (not to speak of Asia); and, supposing it known, what means of conjecturing the weight by which, next year, their fancies, and the changes of style among their jewellers, will diminish or increase it?

the condition at once safest and most convenient* can only be by long analysis, which must for the present be deferred. Gold or silver † may always be retained in limited use, as a luxury of coinage and questionless standard, of one weight and alloy among all nations, varying only in the die. The purity of coinage, when metallic, is closely indicative of the honesty of the system of revenue, and even of the general dignity of the State.‡

78. Whatever the article or articles may be which the national currency promises to pay, a premium on that article indicates bankruptcy of the government in that proportion, the

---

* See, in Pope's epistle to Lord Bathurst, his sketch of the difficulties and uses of a currency literally "pecuniary"—(consisting of herds of cattle).

"His Grace will game—to White's a bull be led," etc.

† Perhaps both; perhaps silver only. It may be found expedient ultimately to leave gold free for use in the arts. As a means of reckoning, the standard might be, and in some cases has already been, entirely ideal.—*See* Mill's *Political Economy*, book iii. chap. VII. at beginning.

‡ The purity of the drachma and zecchin were not without significance of the state of intellect, art, and policy, both in Athens and Venice;—a fact first impressed upon me ten years ago, when, in taking daguerreotypes at Venice, I found no purchaseable gold pure enough to gild them with, except that of the old Venetian zecchin.

division of its assets being restrained only by the remaining confidence of the holders of notes in the return of prosperity to the firm. Currencies of forced acceptance, or of unlimited issue, are merely various modes of disguising taxation, and delaying its pressure, until it is too late to interfere with the cause of pressure. To do away with the possibility of such disguise would have been among the first results of a true economical science, had any such existed; but there have been too many motives for the concealment, so long as it could by any artifices be maintained, to permit hitherto even the founding of such a science.

79. And indeed, it is only through evil conduct, wilfully persisted in, that there is any embarrassment, either in the theory or working of currency. No exchequer is ever embarrassed, nor is any financial question difficult of solution, when people keep their practice honest, and their heads cool. But when governments lose all office of pilotage, protection, or scrutiny; and live only in magnificence of authorized larceny, and polished mendicity; or when the people, choosing Speculation (the *s* usually redundant in the

spelling) instead of Toil, visit no dishonesty with chastisement, that each may with impunity take his dishonest turn;—there are no tricks of financial terminology that will save them; all signature and mintage do but magnify the ruin they retard; and even the riches that remain, stagnant or current, change only from the slime of Avernus to the sand of Phlegethon —*quick*sand at the embouchure;—land fluently recommended by recent auctioneers as "eligible for building leases."

80. Finally, then, the power of true currency is four-fold.

(1.) Credit power. Its worth in exchange, dependent on public opinion of the stability and honesty of the issuer.

(2.) Real worth. Supposing the gold, or whatever else the currency expressly promises, to be required from the issuer, for all his notes; and that the call cannot be met in full. Then the actual worth of the document would be, and its actual worth at any moment is, therefore to be defined as, what the division of the assets of the issuer would produce for it.

(3.) The exchange power of its base. Granting that we can get five pounds in gold for our note, it remains a question how much of other things we can get for five pounds in gold. The more of other things exist, and the less gold, the greater this power.

(4.) The power over labour, exercised by the given quantity of the base, or of the things to be got for it. The question in this case is, how much work, and (question of questions!) *whose* work, is to be had for the food which five pounds will buy. This depends on the number of the population, on their gifts, and on their dispositions, with which, down to their slightest humours, and up to their strongest impulses, the power of the currency varies.

81. Such being the main conditions of national currency, we proceed to examine those of the total currency, under the broad definition, "transferable acknowledgment of debt;"*

---

* Under which term, observe, we include all documents of debt which, being honest, might be transferable, though they practically are not transferred; while we exclude all documents which are in reality worthless, though in fact transferred temporarily, as bad money is. The document of honest debt, not transferred, is merely to paper currency as gold withdrawn from circulation is to that of bullion. Much confusion has crept into the reasoning on this subject from the idea that the withdrawal from circulation is a definable state, whereas it is a graduated state, and

among the many forms of which there are in
effect only two, distinctly opposed; namely,
the acknowledgments of debts which will be
paid, and of debts which will not. Documents,
whether in whole or part, of bad debt, being to
those of good debt as bad money to bullion, we
put for the present these forms of imposture
aside (as in analysing a metal we should wash
it clear of dross), and then range, in their exact

---

indefinable. The sovereign in my pocket is withdrawn from circulation as long as I choose to keep it there. It is no otherwise withdrawn if I bury it, nor even if I choose to make it, and others, into a golden cup, and drink out of them; since a rise in the price of the wine, or of other things, may at any time cause me to melt the cup and throw it back into currency; and the bullion operates on the prices of the things in the market as directly, though not as forcibly, while it is in the form of a cup as it does in the form of a sovereign. No calculation can be founded on my humour in either case. If I like to handle rouleaus, and therefore keep a quantity of gold, to play with, in the form of jointed basaltic columns, it is all one in its effect on the market as if I kept it in the form of twisted filigree, or, steadily "amicus lamnæ," beat the narrow gold pieces into broad ones, and dined off them. The probability is greater that I break the rouleau than that I melt the plate; but the increased probability is not calculable. Thus, documents are only withdrawn from the currency when cancelled, and bullion when it is so effectually lost as that the probability of finding it is no greater than of finding new gold in the mine.

quantities, the true currency of the country on one side, and the store or property of the country on the other. We place gold, and all such substances, on the side of documents, as far as they operate by signature;—on the side of store as far as they operate by value. Then the currency represents the quantity of debt in the country, and the store the quantity of its possession. The ownership of all the property is divided between the holders of currency and holders of store, and whatever the claiming value of the currency is at any moment, that value is to be deducted from the riches of the store-holders.

82. Farther, as true currency represents by definition debts which will be paid, it represents either the debtor's wealth, or his ability and willingness; that is to say, either wealth existing in his hands transferred to him by the creditor, or wealth which, as he is at some time surely to return it, he is either increasing, or, if diminishing, has the will and strength to reproduce. A sound currency therefore, as by its increase it represents enlarging debt, represents also enlarging means; but in this curious way, that a certain quantity of it marks

the deficiency of the wealth of the country from what it would have been if that currency had not existed.* In this respect it is like the detritus of a mountain; assume that it lies at a fixed angle, and the more the detritus, the larger must be the mountain; but it would have been larger still, had there been none.

83. Farther, though, as above stated, every man possessing money has usually also some property beyond what is necessary for his immediate wants, and men possessing property usually also hold currency beyond what is necessary for their immediate exchanges, it

* For example, suppose an active peasant, having got his ground into good order and built himself a comfortable house, finding time still on his hands, sees one of his neighbours little able to work, and ill-lodged, and offers to build him also a house, and to put his land in order, on condition of receiving for a given period rent for the building and tithe of the fruits. The offer is accepted, and a document given promissory of rent and tithe. This note is money. It can only be good money if the man who has incurred the debt so far recovers his strength as to be able to take advantage of the help he has received, and meet the demand of the note; if he lets his house fall to ruin, and his field to waste, his promissory note will soon be valueless: but the existence of the note at all is a consequence of his not having worked so stoutly as the other. Let him gain as much as to be able to pay back the entire debt; the note is cancelled, and we have two rich store-holders and no currency.

mainly determines the class to which they belong, whether in their eyes the money is an adjunct of the property, or the property of the money. In the first case the holder's pleasure is in his possessions, and in his money subordinately, as the means of bettering or adding to them. In the second, his pleasure is in his money, and in his possessions only as representing it. (In the first case the money is as an atmosphere surrounding the wealth, rising from it and raining back upon it; but in the second, it is as a deluge, with the wealth floating, and for the most part perishing in it.*) The shortest distinction between the men is that the one wishes always to buy, and the other to sell.

84. Such being the great relations of the classes, their several characters are of the highest importance to the nation; for on the character of the store-holders chiefly depend the preservation, display, and serviceableness of its wealth ; on that of the currency-holders,

[* You need not trouble yourself to make out the sentence in parenthesis, unless you like, but do not think it is mere metaphor. It states a fact which I could not have stated so shortly, *but* by metaphor.]

its distribution; on that of both, its reproduction.

We shall, therefore, ultimately find it to be of incomparably greater importance to the nation in whose hands the thing is put, than how much of it is got; and that the character of the holders may be conjectured by the quality of the store; for such and such a man always asks for such and such a thing; nor only asks for it, but if it can be bettered, betters it: so that possession and possessor reciprocally act on each other, through the entire sum of national possession. The base nation, asking for base things, sinks daily to deeper vileness of nature and weakness in use; while the noble nation, asking for noble things, rises daily into diviner eminence in both; the tendency to degradation being surely marked by "$\dot{a}\tau a\xi\acute{\iota}a$;" that is to say, (expanding the Greek thought,) by carelessness as to the hands in which things are put, consequent dispute for the acquisition of them, disorderliness in accumulation of them, inaccuracy in estimate of them, and bluntness in conception as to the entire nature of possession.

85. The currency-holders always increase in number and influence in proportion to the bluntness of nature and clumsiness of the store-holders; for the less use people can make of things, the more they want of them, and the sooner weary of them, and want to change them for something else; and all frequency of change increases the quantity and power of currency. The large currency-holder himself is essentially a person who never has been able to make up his mind as to what he will have, and proceeds, therefore, in vague collection and aggregation, with more and more infuriate passion, urged by complacency in progress, vacancy in idea, and pride of conquest.

While, however, there is this obscurity in the nature of possession of currency, there is a charm in the seclusion of it, which is to some people very enticing. In the enjoyment of real property, others must partly share. The groom has some enjoyment of the stud, and the gardener of the garden; but the money is, or seems, shut up; it is wholly enviable. No one else can have part in any complacencies arising from it.

The power of arithmetical comparison is also a great thing to unimaginative people. They know always they are so much better than they were, in money; so much better than others, in money; but wit cannot be so compared, nor character. My neighbour cannot be convinced that I am wiser than he is, but he can, that I am worth so much more; and the universality of the conviction is no less flattering than its clearness. Only a few can understand,—none measure—and few will willingly adore, superiorities in other things; but everybody can understand money, everybody can count it, and most will worship it.

86. Now, these various temptations to accumulation would be politically harmless if what was vainly accumulated had any fair chance of being wisely spent. For as accumulation cannot go on for ever, but must some day end in its reverse—if this reverse were indeed a beneficial distribution and use, as irrigation from reservoir, the fever of gathering, though perilous to the gatherer, might be serviceable to the community. But it constantly happens (so constantly, that it may be stated as a political law having few

exceptions), that what is unreasonably gathered is also unreasonably spent by the persons into whose hands it finally falls. Very frequently it is spent in war, or else in a stupefying luxury, twice hurtful, both in being indulged by the rich and witnessed by the poor. So that the *mal tener* and *mal dare* are as correlative as complementary colours; and the circulation of wealth, which ought to be soft, steady, strong, far-sweeping, and full of warmth, like the Gulf stream, being narrowed into an eddy, and concentrated on a point, changes into the alternate suction and surrender of Charybdis. Which is indeed, I doubt not, the true meaning of that marvellous fable, "infinite," as Bacon said of it, "in matter of meditation." *

87. It is a strange habit of wise humanity to speak in enigmas only, so that the highest truths and usefullest laws must be hunted for through whole picture-galleries of dreams, which to the vulgar seem dreams only. Thus Homer, the Greek tragedians, Plato, Dante,

[* What follows, to the end of the chapter, was a note only, in the first printing; but for after service, it is of more value than any other part of the book, so I have put it into the main text.]

Chaucer, Shakspeare, and Goethe, have hidden all that is chiefly serviceable in their work, and in all the various literature they absorbed and re-embodied, under types which have rendered it quite useless to the multitude. What is worse, the two primal declarers of moral discovery, Homer and Plato, are partly at issue; for Plato's logical power quenched his imagination, and he became incapable of understanding the purely imaginative element either in poetry or painting: he therefore somewhat overrates the pure discipline of passionate art in song and music, and misses that of meditative art. There is, however, a deeper reason for his distrust of Homer. His love of justice, and reverently religious nature, made him dread, as death, every form of fallacy; but chiefly, fallacy respecting the world to come (his own myths being only symbolic exponents of a rational hope). We shall perhaps now every day discover more clearly how right Plato was in this, and feel ourselves more and more wonderstruck that men such as Homer and Dante (and, in an inferior sphere, Milton), not to speak of the great sculptors and painters of every age, have permitted themselves, though full of all nobleness and wisdom, to coin idle imaginations of the mysteries of eternity, and guide the faiths of the families of the earth by the courses of their own vague and visionary arts: while the indisputable truths of human life and duty, respecting which they all have but one voice, lie hidden behind these veils of phantasy, unsought, and often unsuspected. I will gather carefully, out of Dante and Homer, what, in this kind, bears on our subject, in its due place; the first broad intention of their symbols may be sketched at once.

88. The rewards of a worthy use of riches, subordinate to other ends, are shown by Dante in the fifth and sixth orbs of Paradise; for the punishment of their unworthy use, three places are assigned; one for the avaricious and prodigal whose souls are lost (*Hell*, canto 7); one for the avaricious and prodigal whose souls are capable of purification (*Purgatory*, canto 19); and one for the usurers, of whom none can be redeemed (*Hell*, canto 17). The first group, the largest in all hell ("gente piu che altrove troppa," compare Virgil's "quæ maxima turba"), meet in contrary currents,

as the waves of Charybdis, casting weights at each other from opposite sides. This weariness of contention is the chief element of their torture; so marked by the beautiful lines beginning "Or puoi, figliuol," etc.: (but the usurers, who made their money inactively, *sit* on the sand, equally without rest, however. "Di qua, di la, soccorrien," etc.) For it is not avarice, but *contention* for riches, leading to this double misuse of them, which, in Dante's light, is the unredeemable sin. The place of its punishment is guarded by Plutus, "the great enemy," and "la fiera crudele," a spirit quite different from the Greek Plutus, who, though old and blind, is not cruel, and is curable, so as to become far-sighted. (οὐ τυφλὸς ἀλλ' ὀξὺ βλέπων.—Plato's epithets in first book of the *Laws.*) Still more does this Dantesque type differ from the resplendent Plutus of Goethe in the second part of *Faust,* who is the personified power of wealth for good or evil—not the passion for wealth; and again from the Plutus of Spenser, who is the passion of mere aggregation. Dante's Plutus is specially and definitely the Spirit of Contention and Competition, or Evil Commerce;

because, as I showed before, this kind of commerce "makes all men strangers;" his speech is therefore unintelligible, and no single soul of all those ruined by him *has recognizable features*.

On the other hand, the redeemable sins of avarice and prodigality are, in Dante's sight, those which are without deliberate or calculated operation. The lust, or lavishness, of riches can be purged, so long as there has been no servile consistency of dispute and competition for them. The sin is spoken of as that of degradation by the love of earth; it is purified by deeper humiliation—the souls crawl on their bellies; their chant is, "my soul cleaveth unto the dust." But the spirits thus condemned are all recognizable, and even the worst examples of the thirst for gold, which they are compelled to tell the histories of during the night, are of men swept by the passion of avarice into violent crime, but not sold to its steady work.

89. The precept given to each of these spirits for its deliverance is—Turn thine eyes to the lucre (lure) which the Eternal King rolls with the mighty wheels. Otherwise,

the wheels of the "Greater Fortune," of which the constellation is ascending when Dante's dream begins. Compare George Herbert—

> "Lift up thy head ;
> Take stars for money ; stars, not to be told
> By any art, yet to be purchased."

And Plato's notable sentence in the third book of the *Polity*:—"Tell them they have divine gold and silver in their souls for ever; that they need no money stamped of men—neither may they otherwise than impiously mingle the gathering of the divine with the mortal treasure, *for through that which the law of the multitude has coined, endless crimes have been done and suffered; but in theirs is neither pollution nor sorrow.*"

90. At the entrance of this place of punishment an evil spirit is seen by Dante, quite other than the "Gran Nemico." The great enemy is obeyed knowingly and willingly; but the spirit—feminine—and called a Siren—is the "*Deceitfulness* of riches," ἀπάτη πλούτου of the Gospels, winning obedience by guile. This is the Idol of riches, made doubly phantasmal by Dante's seeing her in a dream. She is lovely to look upon, and enchants by

her sweet singing, but her womb is loathsome. Now, Dante does not call her one of the Sirens carelessly, any more than he speaks of Charybdis carelessly; and though he had got at the meaning of Homeric fable only through Virgil's obscure tradition of it, the clue he has given us is quite enough. Bacon's interpretation, "the Sirens, *or pleasures,*" which has become universal since his time, is opposed alike to Plato's meaning and Homer's. The Sirens are not pleasures, but *Desires:* in the Odyssey they are the phantoms of vain desire; but in Plato's Vision of Destiny, phantoms of divine desire; singing each a different note on the circles of the distaff of Necessity, but forming one harmony, to which the three great Fates put words. Dante, however, adopted the Homeric conception of them, which was that they were demons of the Imagination, not carnal; (desire of the eyes; not lust of the flesh;) therefore said to be daughters of the Muses. Yet not of the Muses, heavenly or historical, but of the Muse of pleasure; and they are at first winged, because even vain hope excites and helps when first formed; but afterwards, contending for the possession of the imagination with the Muses themselves, they are deprived of their wings.

91. And thus we are to distinguish the Siren power from the power of Circe, who is no daughter of the Muses, but of the strong elements, Sun and Sea; her power is that of frank, and full vital pleasure, which, if governed and watched, nourishes men; but, unwatched, and having no "moly," bitterness or delay, mixed with it, turns men into beasts, but does not slay them,—leaves them, on the contrary, power of revival. She is herself indeed an Enchantress;—pure Animal life; transforming—or degrading—but always wonderful (she puts the stores on board the ship invisibly, and is gone again, like a ghost); even the wild beasts rejoice and are softened around her cave; the transforming poisons she gives to men are mixed with no rich feast, but with pure and right nourishment,— Pramnian wine, cheese, and flour; that is, wine, milk, and corn, the three great sustainers of life—it is their own fault if these make swine of them; (see Appendix V.) and swine are chosen merely as the type of consumption; as Plato's ὑῶν πόλις, in the second book of

the *Polity*, and perhaps chosen by Homer with a deeper knowledge of the likeness in variety of nourishment, and internal form of body.

"Et quel est, s'il vous plait, cet audacieux animal qui se permet d'être bâti au dedans comme une jolie petite fille ?

"Hélas! chère enfant, j'ai honte de le nommer, et il ne faudra pas m'en vouloir. C'est . . . c'est le cochon. Ce n'est pas précisément flatteur pour vous ; mais nous en sommes tout là, et si cela vous contrarie par trop, il faut aller vous plaindre au bon Dieu qui a voulu que les choses fussent arrangées ainsi: seulement le cochon, qui ne pense qu'à manger, a l'estomac bien plus vaste que nous et c'est toujours une consolation."—*Histoire d'une Bouchée de Pain*, Lettre ix.)

92. But the deadly Sirens are in all things opposed to the Circean power. They promise pleasure, but never give it. They nourish in no wise; but slay by slow death. And whereas they corrupt the heart and the head, instead of merely betraying the senses, there is no recovery from their power; they do not tear nor scratch, like Scylla, but the men who have listened to them are poisoned, and waste

away. Note that the Sirens' field is covered, not merely with the bones, but with the *skins*, of those who have been consumed there. They address themselves, in the part of the song which Homer gives, not to the passions of Ulysses, but to his vanity, and the only man who ever came within hearing of them, and escaped untempted, was Orpheus, who silenced the vain imaginations by singing the praises of the gods.

93. It is, then, one of these Sirens whom Dante takes as the phantasm or deceitfulness of riches; but note further, that she says it was her song that deceived Ulysses. Look back to Dante's account of Ulysses' death, and we find it was not the love of money, but pride of knowledge, that betrayed him; whence we get the clue to Dante's complete meaning: that the souls whose love of wealth is pardonable have been first deceived into pursuit of it by a dream of its higher uses, or by ambition. His Siren is therefore the Philotimé of Spenser, daughter of Mammon—

> "Whom all that folk with such contention
> Do flock about, my deare, my daughter is—
> Honour and dignitie from her alone
> Derived are."

By comparing Spenser's entire account of this Philotimé with Dante's of the Wealth-Siren, we shall get at the full meaning of both poets; but that of Homer lies hidden much more deeply. For his Sirens are indefinite; and they are desires of any evil thing; power of wealth is not specially indicated by him, until, escaping the harmonious danger of imagination, Ulysses has to choose between two *practical ways of life,* indicated by the two *rocks* of Scylla and Charybdis. The monsters that haunt them are quite distinct from the rocks themselves, which, having many other subordinate significations, are in the main Labour and Idleness, or getting and spending; each with its attendant monster, or betraying demon. The rock of gaining has its summit in the clouds, invisible, and not to be climbed; that of spending is low, but marked by the cursed fig-tree, which has leaves, but no fruit. We know the type elsewhere; and there is a curious lateral allusion to it by Dante when Jacopo di Sant' Andrea, who had ruined himself by profusion and committed suicide, scatters the leaves of the bush of Lotto degli Agli, endeavouring to hide himself among them. We shall hereafter examine the type completely; here I will only give an approximate rendering of Homer's words, which have been obscured more by translation than even by tradition.

94. "They are overhanging rocks. The great waves of blue water break round them; and the blessed Gods call them the Wanderers.

"By one of them no winged thing can pass —not even the wild doves that bring ambrosia to their father Jove—but the smooth rock seizes its sacrifice of them." (Not even ambrosia to be had without Labour. The word is peculiar—as a part of anything is offered for sacrifice; especially used of heave-offering.) "It reaches the wide heaven with its top, and a dark-blue cloud rests on it, and never passes; neither does the clear sky hold it, in summer nor in harvest. Nor can any man climb it—not if he had twenty feet and hands, for it is as smooth as though it were hewn.

"And in the midst of it is a cave which is turned the way of hell. And therein dwells Scylla, whining for prey; her cry, indeed, is no louder than that of a newly-born whelp:

but she herself is an awful thing—nor can any creature see her face and be glad; no, though it were a god that rose against her. For she had twelve feet, all fore-feet, and six necks, and terrible heads on them; and each has three rows of teeth, full of black death.

"But the opposite rock is lower than this, though but a bow-shot distant; and upon it there is a great fig-tree, full of leaves; and under it the terrible Charybdis sucks down the black water. Thrice in the day she sucks it down, and thrice casts it up again; be not thou there when she sucks down, for Neptune himself could not save thee."

[Thus far went my rambling note, in *Fraser's Magazine*. The Editor sent me a compliment on it—of which I was very proud; what the Publisher thought of it, I am not informed; only I know that eventually he stopped the papers. I think a great deal of it myself, now, and have put it all in large print accordingly, and should like to write more; but will, on the contrary, self-denyingly, and in gratitude to any reader who has got through so much, end my chapter.]

CHAPTER IV.

COMMERCE.

95. As the currency conveys right of choice out of many things in exchange for one, so Commerce is the agency by which the power of choice is obtained; so that countries producing only timber can obtain for their timber silk and gold; or, naturally producing only jewels and frankincense, can obtain for them cattle and corn. In this function, commerce is of more importance to a country in proportion to the limitations of its products, and the restlessness of its fancy;—generally of greater importance towards Northern latitudes.

96. Commerce is necessary, however, not only to exchange local products, but local skill. Labour requiring the agency of fire can only be given abundantly in cold countries; labour requiring suppleness of body and sensitiveness of touch, only in warm ones; labour

involving accurate vivacity of thought only in temperate ones; while peculiar imaginative actions are produced by extremes of heat and cold, and of light and darkness. The production of great art is limited to climates warm enough to admit of repose in the open air, and cool enough to render such repose delightful. Minor variations in modes of skill distinguish every locality. The labour which at any place is easiest, is in that place cheapest; and it becomes often desirable that products raised in one country should be wrought in another. Hence have arisen discussions on "International values" which will be one day remembered as highly curious exercises of the human mind. For it will be discovered, in due course of tide and time, that international value is regulated just as inter-provincial or inter-parishional value is. Coals and hops are exchanged between Northumberland and Kent on absolutely the same principles as iron and wine between Lancashire and Spain. The greater breadth of an arm of the sea increases the cost, but does not modify the principle of exchange; and a bargain written in two languages will have no other economical results than a bargain written in one. The distances of nations are measured, not by seas, but by ignorances; and their divisions determined, not by dialects, but by enmities.*

97. Of course, a system of international values may always be constructed if we assume a relation of moral law to physical geography; as, for instance, that it is right to cheat or rob across a river, though not across a road; or across a sea, though not across a river, etc.; —again, a system of such values may be constructed by assuming similar relations of taxation to physical geography; as, for instance, that an article should be taxed in crossing a river, but not in crossing a road; or in being carried fifty miles, but not in being carried five, etc.; such positions are indeed not easily maintained when once put in logical form; but *one* law of international value is maintainable

[* I have repeated the substance of this and the next paragraph so often since, that I am ashamed and weary. The thing is too true, and too simple, it seems, for anybody ever to believe. Meantime, the theories of "international values," as explained by Modern Political Economy, have brought about last year's pillage of France by Germany, and the affectionate relations now existing in consequence between the inhabitants of the right and left banks of the Rhine.]

in any form: namely, that the farther your neighbour lives from you, and the less he understands you, *the more you are bound to be true in your dealings with him;* because your power over him is greater in proportion to his ignorance, and his remedy more difficult in proportion to his distance.*

98. I have just said the breadth of sea increases the cost of exchange. Now note that exchange, or commerce, *in itself*, is always costly; the sum of the value of the goods being diminished by the cost of their conveyance, and by the maintenance of the persons employed in it; so that it is only when there is advantage to both producers (in getting the one thing for the other) greater than the loss in conveyance, that the exchange is expedient. And it can only be justly conducted when the porters kept by the producers (commonly called merchants) expect *mere* pay, and not profit.† For in just commerce there are but three parties—the two persons or

[* I wish some one would examine and publish accurately the late dealings of the Governors of the Cape with the Caffirs.]

[† By "pay," I mean wages for labour or skill; by "profit," gain dependent on the state of the market.]

societies exchanging, and the agent or agents of exchange; the value of the things to be exchanged is known by both the exchangers, and each receives equal value, neither gaining nor losing (for whatever one gains the other loses). The intermediate agent is paid a known per-centage by both, partly for labour in conveyance, partly for care, knowledge, and risk; every attempt at concealment of the amount of the pay indicates either effort on the part of the agent to obtain unjust profit, or effort on the part of the exchangers to refuse him just pay. But for the most part it is the first, namely the effort on the part of the merchant to obtain larger profit (so-called) by buying cheap and selling dear. Some part, indeed, of this larger gain is deserved, and might be openly demanded, because it is the reward of the merchant's knowledge, and foresight of probable necessity; but the greater part of such gain is unjust; and unjust in this most fatal way, that it depends, first, on keeping the exchangers ignorant of the exchange value of the articles; and, secondly, on taking advantage of the buyer's need and the seller's poverty. It is, therefore, one of the essential, and quite the most fatal, forms of usury; for usury means merely taking an exorbitant* sum for the use of anything; and it is no matter whether the exorbitance is on loan or exchange, on rent or on price—the essence of the usury being that it is obtained by advantage of opportunity or necessity, and not as due reward for labour. All the great thinkers, therefore, have held it to be unnatural and impious, in so far as it feeds on the distress of others, or their folly.† Nevertheless, attempts to repress it by law must for ever be ineffective; though Plato, Bacon, and the First Napoleon—all three of them men who knew somewhat more of humanity than the "British merchant" usually does—tried their hands at it, and have left

[* Since I wrote this, I have worked out the question of interest of money, which always, until lately, had embarrassed and defeated me; and I find that the payment of interest of any amount whatever is real "usury," and entirely unjustifiable. I was shown this chiefly by the pamphlets issued by Mr. W. C. Sillar, though I greatly regret the impatience which causes Mr. Sillar to regard usury as the radical crime in political economy. There are others worse, that act with it.]

† Hence Dante's companionship of Cahors, *Inf.*, canto xi., supported by the view taken of the matter throughout the Middle Ages, in common with the Greeks.

some (probably) good moderative forms of law, which we will examine in their place. But the only final check upon it must be radical purifying of the national character, for being, as Bacon calls it, "concessum propter duritiem cordis," it is to be done away with by touching the heart only; not, however, without medicinal law—as in the case of the other permission, "propter duritiem." But in this more than in anything (though much in all, and though in this he would not himself allow of their application, for his own laws against usury are sharp enough), Plato's words in the fourth book of the *Polity* are true, that neither drugs, nor charms, nor burnings, will touch a deep-lying political sore, any more than a deep bodily one; but only right and utter change of constitution: and that "they do but lose their labour who think that by any tricks of law they can get the better of these mischiefs of commerce, and see not that they hew at a Hydra."

99. And indeed this Hydra seems so unslayable, and sin sticks so fast between the joinings of the stones of buying and selling, that "to trade" in things, or literally "cross-give"

them, has warped itself, by the instinct of nations, into their worst word for fraud; for, because in trade there cannot but be trust, and it seems also that there cannot but also be injury in answer to it, what is merely fraud between enemies becomes treachery among friends: and " trader," " traditor," and " traitor" are but the same word. For which simplicity of language there is more reason than at first appears; for as in true commerce there is no " profit," so in true commerce there is no " sale." The idea of sale is that of an interchange between enemies respectively endeavouring to get the better one of another; but commerce is an exchange between friends; and there is no desire but that it should be just, any more than there would be between members of the same family.* The moment there is a bargain over the pottage, the family relation is dissolved:—typically, " the days of mourning for my father are at hand."

[* I do not wonder when I re-read this, that people talk about my "sentiment." But there is no sentiment whatever in the matter. It is a hard and bare commercial fact, that if two people deal together who don't try to cheat each other, they will, in a given time, make more money out of each other than if they do. See § 104.]

Whereupon follows the resolve, "then will I slay my brother."

100. This inhumanity of mercenary commerce is the more notable because it is a fulfilment of the law that the corruption of the best is the worst. For as, taking the body natural for symbol of the body politic, the governing and forming powers may be likened to the brain, and the labouring to the limbs, the mercantile, presiding over circulation and communication of things in changed utilities, is symbolized by the heart; and, if that hardens, all is lost. And this is the ultimate lesson which the leader of English intellect meant for us, (a lesson, indeed, not all his own, but part of the old wisdom of humanity,) in the tale of the *Merchant of Venice;* in which the true and incorrupt merchant,—*kind and free, beyond every other Shakspearian conception of men,*—is opposed to the corrupted merchant, or usurer; the lesson being deepened by the expression of the strange hatred which the corrupted merchant bears to the pure one, mixed with intense scorn,—

"This is the fool that lent out money

gratis; look to him, jailor," (as to lunatic no less than criminal) the enmity, observe, having its symbolism literally carried out by being aimed straight at the heart, and finally foiled by a literal appeal to the great moral law that flesh and blood cannot be weighed, enforced by "Portia"* ("Portion"), the type of divine Fortune, found, not in gold, nor in silver, but

---

* Shakspeare would certainly never have chosen this name had he been forced to retain the Roman spelling. Like Perdita, "lost lady," or Cordelia, "heart-lady," Portia is "fortune" lady. The two great relative groups of words, Fortuna, fero, and fors—Portio, porto, and pars (with the lateral branch op-portune, im-portune, opportunity, etc.), are of deep and intricate significance; their various senses of bringing, abstracting, and sustaining being all centralized by the wheel (which bears and moves at once), or still better, the ball (spera) of fortune,—" Volve sua spera, e beata si gode:" the motive power of this wheel distinguishing its goddess from the fixed majesty of Necessitas with her iron nails; or ἀνάγκη, with her pillar of fire and iridescent orbits, *fixed* at the centre. Portus and porta, and gate in its connexion with gain, form another interesting branch group; and Mors, the concentration of delaying, is always to be remembered with Fors, the concentration of bringing and bearing, passing on into Fortis and Fortitude.

[This note is literally a mere memorandum for the future work which I am now completing in *Fors Clavigera*; it was printed partly in vanity, but also with real desire to get people to share the interest I found in the careful study of the leading words in noble languages. Compare the next note.]

in lead, that is to say, in endurance and patience, not in splendour; and finally taught by her lips also, declaring, instead of the law and quality of "merces," the greater law and quality of mercy, which is not strained, but drops as the rain, blessing him that gives and him that takes. And observe that this "mercy" is not the mean "Misericordia," but the mighty "Gratia," answered by Gratitude, (observe Shylock's learning on the, to him detestable, word, *gratis*, and compare the relations of Grace to Equity given in the second chapter of the second book of the *Memorabilia*;) that is to say, it is the gracious or loving, instead of the strained, or competing manner, of doing things, answered, not only with "merces" or pay, but with "merci" or thanks. And this is indeed the meaning of the great benediction "Grace, mercy, and peace," for there can be no peace without grace, (not even by help of rifled cannon,) nor even without triplicity of graciousness, for the Greeks, who began but with one Grace, had to open their scheme into three before they had done.

101. With the usual tendency of long

repeated thought, to take the surface for the deep, we have conceived these goddesses as if they only gave loveliness to gesture; whereas their true function is to give graciousness to deed, the other loveliness arising naturally out of that. In which function Charis becomes Charitas;* and has a name and praise even greater than that of Faith or Truth, for these may be maintained sullenly and proudly; but Charis is in her countenance always gladdening (Aglaia), and in her service instant and humble; and the true wife of Vulcan, or Labour. And it is not until her sincerity of function is lost, and her mere beauty

---

* As Charis becomes Charitas, the word "Cher," or "Dear," passes from Shylock's sense of it (to buy cheap and sell dear) into Antonio's sense of it: emphasized with the final *i* in tender "Cheri," and hushed to English calmness in our noble "Cherish." The reader must not think that any care can be misspent in tracing the connexion and power of the words which we have to use in the sequel. (See Appendix VI.) Much education sums itself in making men economize their words, and understand them. Nor is it possible to estimate the harm which has been done, in matters of higher speculation and conduct, by loose verbiage, though we may guess at it by observing the dislike which people show to having anything about their religion said to them in simple words, because then they understand it. Thus congregations meet weekly to invoke the influence of a

contemplated instead of her patience, that she is born again of the foam flake, and becomes Aphrodite; and it is then only that she becomes capable of joining herself to war and to the enmities of men, instead of to labour and their services. Therefore the fable of Mars and Venus is chosen by Homer, picturing himself as Demodocus, to sing at the games in the court of Alcinous. Phæacia is the Homeric island of Atlantis; an image of noble and wise government, concealed, (how slightly!) merely by the change of a short vowel for a long one in the name of its queen; yet misunderstood by all later writers, (even by Horace, in his "pinguis, Phæaxque").

Spirit of Life and Truth; yet if any part of that character were intelligibly expressed to them by the formulas of the service, they would be offended. Suppose, for instance, in the closing benediction, the clergyman were to give vital significance to the vague word "Holy," and were to say, "the fellowship of the Helpful and Honest Ghost be with you, and remain with you always," what would be the horror of many, first at the irreverence of so intelligible an expression; and secondly, at the discomfortable occurrence of the suspicion that while throughout the commercial dealings of the week they had denied the propriety of Help, and possibility of Honesty, the Person whose company they had been now asking to be blessed with could have no fellowship with cruel people or knaves.

That fable expresses the perpetual error of men in thinking that grace and dignity can only be reached by the soldier, and never by the artizan; so that commerce and the useful arts have had the honour and beauty taken away, and only the Fraud and Pain left to them, with the lucre. Which is, indeed, one great reason of the continual blundering about the offices of government with respect to commerce. The higher classes are ashamed to employ themselves in it; and though ready enough to fight for (or occasionally against) the people,—to preach to them,—or judge them, will not break bread for them; the refined upper servant who has willingly looked after the burnishing of the armoury and ordering of the library, not liking to set foot in the larder.

102. Farther still. As Charis becomes Charitas on the one side, she becomes— better still—Chara, Joy, on the other; or rather this is her very mother's milk and the beauty of her childhood; for God brings no enduring Love, nor any other good, out of pain; nor out of contention; but out of joy and harmony. And in this sense, human and

divine, music and gladness, and the measures of both, come into her name; and Cher becomes full-vowelled Cheer, and Cheerful; and Chara opens into Choir and Choral.*

103. And lastly. As Grace passes into Freedom of action, Charis becomes Eleutheria, or Liberality; a form of liberty quite curiously and intensely different from the thing usually understood by "Liberty" in modern language: indeed, much more like what some people would call slavery: for a Greek always understood, primarily, by liberty, deliverance from the law of his own passions (or from what the Christian writers call bondage of corruption),

---

* "τὰ μὲν οὖν ἄλλα ζῶα οὐκ ἔχειν αἴσθησιν τῶν ἐν ταῖς κινήσεσι τάξεων οὐδὲ ἀταξιῶν, οἷς δὴ ῥυθμὸς ὄνομα καὶ ἁρμονία· ἡμῖν δὲ οὓς εἴπομεν τοὺς θεοὺς (Apollo, the Muses, and Bacchus—the grave Bacchus, that is—ruling the choir of age; or Bacchus restraining; 'sæva tene, cum Berecyntio cornu, tympana,' etc.) συγχορευτὰς δεδόσθαι, τούτους εἶναι καὶ τοὺς δεδωκότας τὴν ἔνρυθμόν τε καὶ ἐναρμόνιον αἴσθησιν μεθ' ἡδονῆς ... χόρους τε ὠνομακέναι παρὰ τῆς χαρᾶς ἔμφυτον ὄνομα." "Other animals have no perception of order nor of disorder in motion; but for us, Apollo and Bacchus and the Muses are appointed to mingle in our dances; and these are they who have given us the sense of delight in rhythm and harmony. And the name of choir, choral dance, (we may believe,) came from chara (delight)."—*Laws*, book ii.

and this a complete liberty: not being merely safe from the Siren, but also unbound from the mast, and not having to resist the passion, but making it fawn upon, and follow him—(this may be again partly the meaning of the fawning beasts about the Circean cave; so, again, George Herbert—

> Correct thy passion's spite,
> Then may the beasts draw thee to happy light)—

And it is only in such generosity that any man becomes capable of so governing others as to take true part in any system of national economy. Nor is there any other eternal distinction between the upper and lower classes than this form of liberty, Eleutheria, or benignity, in the one, and its opposite of slavery, Douleia, or malignity, in the other; the separation of these two orders of men, and the firm government of the lower by the higher, being the first conditions of possible wealth and economy in any State,—the Gods giving it no greater gift than the power to discern its true freemen, and "malignum spernere vulgus."

104. While I have traced the finer and

higher laws of this matter for those whom they concern, I have also to note the material law—vulgarly expressed in the proverb, "Honesty is the best policy." That proverb is indeed wholly inapplicable to matters of private interest. It is not true that honesty, as far as material gain is concerned, profits individuals. A clever and cruel knave will in a mixed society always be richer than an honest person can be. But Honesty is the best "policy," if policy mean practice of State. For fraud gains nothing in a State. It only enables the knaves in it to live at the expense of honest people; while there is for every act of fraud, however small, a loss of wealth to the community. Whatever the fraudulent person gains, some other person loses, as fraud produces nothing; and there is, *besides*, the loss of the time and thought spent in accomplishing the fraud, and of the strength otherwise obtainable by mutual help (not to speak of the fevers of anxiety and jealousy in the blood, which are a heavy physical loss, as I will show in due time). Practically, when the nation is deeply corrupt, cheat answers to cheat; every one is in turn imposed upon, and there is to the body politic the dead loss of the ingenuity, together with the incalculable mischief of the injury to each defrauded person, producing collateral effect unexpectedly. My neighbour sells me bad meat: I sell him in return flawed iron. We neither of us get one atom of pecuniary advantage on the whole transaction, but we both suffer unexpected inconvenience; my men get scurvy, and his cattle-truck runs off the rails.

105. The examination of this form of Charis must, therefore, lead us into the discussion of the principles of government in general, and especially of that of the poor by the rich, discovering how the Graciousness joined with the Greatness, or Love with Majestas, is the true Dei Gratia, or Divine Right, of every form and manner of King; *i.e.,* specifically, of the thrones, dominations, princedoms, virtues, and powers of the earth:—of the thrones, stable, or "ruling," literally rightdoing powers ("rex eris, recte si facies"):— of the dominations—lordly, edifying, dominant and harmonious powers; chiefly domestic, over the "built thing," domus, or house; and inherently twofold, Dominus and Domina; Lord and Lady:—of the Princedoms, pre-eminent,

incipient, creative, and demonstrative powers; thus poetic and mercantile, in the "princeps carmen deduxisse" and the merchant-prince:—of the Virtues or Courages; militant, guiding, or Ducal powers:—and finally of the Strengths, or Forces pure; magistral powers, of the More over the less, and the forceful and free over the weak and servile elements of life.

Subject enough for the next paper, involving "economical" principles of some importance, of which, for theme, here is a sentence, which I do not care to translate, for it would sound harsh in English,* though, truly, it is one of the tenderest ever uttered by man; which may be meditated over, or rather *through*, in the meanwhile, by any one who will take the pains:—

Ἆρ' οὖν, ὥσπερ ἵππος τῷ ἀνεπιστήμονι μὲν ἐγχειροῦντι δὲ χρῆσθαι ζημία ἐστὶν, οὕτω καὶ ἀδελφὸς, ὅταν τις αὐτῷ μὴ ἐπιστάμενος ἐγχειρῇ χρῆσθαι. ζημία ἐστί;

[* My way now, is to say things plainly, if I can, whether they sound harsh or not;—this is the translation—"Is it possible, then, that as a horse is only a mischief to any one who attempts to use him without knowing how, so also our brother, if we attempt to use him without knowing how, may be a mischief to us?"]

CHAPTER V.

GOVERNMENT.

106. It remains for us, as I stated in the close of the last chapter, to examine first the principles of government in general, and then those of the government of the Poor by the Rich.

The government of a state consists in its customs, laws, and councils, and their enforcements.

I. Customs.

As one person primarily differs from another by fineness of nature, and, secondarily, by fineness of training, so also, a polite nation differs from a savage one, first, by the refinement of its nature, and secondly by the delicacy of its customs.

In the completeness of custom, which is the nation's self-government, there are three stages—first, fineness in method of doing or of being;—called the manner or moral of acts; secondly, firmness in holding such method after adoption, so that it shall become a habit in the character: *i.e.*, a constant "having" or "behaving;" and, lastly, ethical power in performance and endurance, which is the skill following on habit, and the ease reached by frequency of right doing.

The sensibility of the nation is indicated by the fineness of its customs; its courage, continence, and self-respect by its persistence in them.

By sensibility I mean its natural perception of beauty, fitness, and rightness; or of what is lovely, decent, and just: faculties dependent much on race, and the primal signs of fine breeding in man; but cultivable also by education, and necessarily perishing without it. True education has, indeed, no other function than the development of these faculties, and of the relative will. It has been the great error of modern intelligence to mistake science for education. You do not educate a man by telling him what he knew not, but by making him what he was not.

And making him what he will remain for ever: for no wash of weeds will bring back the faded purple. And in that dyeing there are two processes—first, the cleansing and wringing-out, which is the baptism with water; and then the infusing of the blue and scarlet colours, gentleness and justice, which is the baptism with fire.

107.* The customs and manners of a sensitive and highly-trained race are always Vital: that is to say, they are orderly manifestations of intense life, like the habitual action of the fingers of a musician. The customs and manners of a vile and rude race, on the contrary, are conditions of decay: they are not, properly speaking, habits, but incrustations; not restraints, or forms, of life; but gangrenes, noisome, and the beginnings of death.

And generally, so far as custom attaches itself to indolence instead of action, and to prejudice instead of perception, it takes this deadly character, so that thus

> Custom hangs upon us with a weight
> Heavy as frost, and deep almost as life.

[* Think over this paragraph carefully; it should have

But that weight, if it becomes impetus, (living instead of dead weight) is just what gives value to custom, when it works *with* life, instead of against it.

108. The high ethical training of a nation implies perfect Grace, Pitifulness, and Peace; it is irreconcilably inconsistent with filthy or mechanical employments,—with the desire of money,—and with mental states of anxiety, jealousy, or indifference to pain. The present insensibility of the upper classes of Europe to the surrounding aspects of suffering, uncleanness, and crime, binds them not only into one responsibility with the sin, but into one dishonour with the foulness, which rot at their thresholds. The crimes daily recorded in the police-courts of London and Paris (and much more those which are *un*recorded) are a disgrace to the whole body politic;* they are,

been much expanded to be quite intelligible; but it contains all that I want it to contain.]

* "The ordinary brute, who flourishes in the very centre of ornate life, tells us of unknown depths on the verge of which we totter, being bound to thank our stars every day we live that there is not a general outbreak, and a revolt from the yoke of civilization."—*Times* leader, Dec. 25, 1862. Admitting that our stars are to be thanked for our safety, whom are we to thank for the danger?

as in the body natural, stains of disease on a face of delicate skin, making the delicacy itself frightful. Similarly, the filth and poverty permitted or ignored in the midst of us are as dishonourable to the whole social body, as in the body natural it is to wash the face, but leave the hands and feet foul. Christ's way is the only true one: begin at the feet; the face will take care of itself.

109. Yet, since necessarily, in the frame of a nation, nothing but the head can be of gold, and the feet, for the work they have to do, must be part of iron, part of clay;—foul or mechanical work is always reduced by a noble race to the minimum in quantity; and, even then, performed and endured, not without sense of degradation, as a fine temper is wounded by the sight of the lower offices of the body. The highest conditions of human society reached hitherto have cast such work to slaves; but supposing slavery of a politically defined kind to be done away with, mechanical and foul employment must, in all highly organised states, take the aspect either of punishment or probation. All criminals should at once be set to the most dangerous and

painful forms of it, especially to work in mines and at furnaces,* so as to relieve the innocent population as far as possible: of merely rough (not mechanical) manual labour, especially agricultural, *a large portion should be done by the upper classes;—bodily health, and sufficient contrast and repose for the mental functions, being unattainable without it;* what necessarily inferior labour remains to be done,

---

* Our politicians, even the best of them, regard only the distress caused by the *failure* of mechanical labour. The degradation caused by its excess is a far more serious subject of thought, and of future fear. I shall examine this part of our subject at length hereafter. There can hardly be any doubt, at present, cast on the truth of the above passages, as all the great thinkers are unanimous on the matter. Plato's words are terrific in their scorn and pity whenever he touches on the mechanical arts. He calls the men employed in them not even human, but partially and diminutively human, "ἀνθρωπίσκοι," and opposes such work to noble occupations, not merely as prison is opposed to freedom, but as a convict's dishonoured prison is to the temple (escape from them being like that of a criminal to the sanctuary); and the destruction caused by them being of soul no less than body.—*Rep.* vi. 9. Compare *Laws*, v. 11. Xenophon dwells on the evil of occupations at the furnace, and especially their "ἀσχολία, want of leisure."—*Econ.* i. 4. (Modern England, with all its pride of education, has lost that first sense of the word "school;" and till it recover that, it will find no other rightly.) His word for the harm to the soul is to "break" it, as we say of the heart.—*Econ.* i. 6. And herein, also, is the root of the scorn, otherwise apparently

as especially in manufactures, should, and always will, when the relations of society are reverent and harmonious, fall to the lot of those who, for the time, are fit for nothing better. For as, whatever the perfectness of the educational system, there must remain infinite differences between the natures and capacities of men; and these differing natures are generally rangeable under the two qualities most strange and cruel, with which Homer, Dante, and Shakspeare always speak of the populace; for it is entirely true that, in great states, the lower orders are low by nature as well as by task, being precisely that part of the commonwealth which has been thrust down for its coarseness or unworthiness (by coarseness I mean especially insensibility and irreverence—the "profane" of Horace); and when this ceases to be so, and the corruption and profanity are in the higher instead of the lower orders, there arises, first helpless confusion; then, if the lower classes deserve power, ensues swift revolution, and they get it; but if neither the populace nor their rulers deserve it, there follows mere darkness and dissolution, till, out of the putrid elements, some new capacity of order rises, like grass on a grave; if not, there is no more hope, nor shadow of turning, for that nation. Atropos has her way with it.

So that the law of national health is like that of a great lake or sea, in perfect but slow circulation, letting the dregs fall continually to the lowest place, and the clear water rise; yet so as that there shall be no neglect of the lower orders, but perfect supervision and sympathy, so that if one member suffer, all members shall suffer with it.

of lordly, (or tending towards rule, construction, and harmony), and servile (or tending towards misrule, destruction, and discord); and, since the lordly part is only in a state of profitableness while ruling, and the servile only in a state of redeemableness while serving, the whole health of the state depends on the manifest separation of these two elements of its mind; for, if the servile part be not separated and rendered visible in service, it mixes with, and corrupts, the entire body of the state; and if the lordly part be not distinguished, and set to rule, it is crushed and lost, being turned to no account, so that the rarest qualities of the nation are all given to it in vain. *

II. LAWS.

110. These are the definitions and bonds of custom, or of what the nation desires should become custom.

Law is either archic,† (of direction), meristic, (of division), or critic, (of judgment).

---

* "ὀλίγης, καὶ ἄλλως γιγνομένης." (Little, and that little born in vain.) The bitter sentence never was so true as at this day.

† [This following note is a mere cluster of memoranda,

Archic law is that of appointment and precept: it defines what is and is not to be *done.*

Meristic law is that of balance and distribution: it defines what is and is not to be *possessed.*

Critic law is that of discernment and award: it defines what is and is not to be *suffered.*

III. A. ARCHIC LAW. If we choose to unite the laws of precept and distribution under the head of " statutes," all law is simply either of statute or judgment; that is, first the establishment of ordinance, and, secondly, the

but I keep it for reference.] Thetic, or Thesmic, would perhaps be a better term than archic; but liable to be confused with some which we shall want relating to Theoria. The administrators of the three great divisions of law are severally Archons, Merists, and Dicasts. The Archons are the true princes, or beginners of things ; or leaders (as of an orchestra). The Merists are properly the Domini, or Lords of houses and nations. The Dicasts, properly, the judges, and that with Olympian justice, which reaches to heaven and hell. The violation of archic law is ἁμαρτία (error), πονηρία (failure), or πλημμέλεια (discord). The violation of meristic law is ἀνομία (iniquity). The violation of critic law is ἀδικία (injury). Iniquity is the central generic term ; for all law is *fatal;* it is the division to men of their fate ; as the fold of their pasture, it is νόμος ; as the assigning of their portion, μοῖρα.

assignment of the reward, or penalty, due to its observance or violation.

To some extent these two forms of law must be associated, and, with every ordinance, the penalty of disobedience to it be also determined. But since the degrees and guilt of disobedience vary, the determination of due reward and punishment must be modified by discernment of special fact, which is peculiarly the office of the judge, as distinguished from that of the lawgiver and law-sustainer, or king; not but that the two offices are always theoretically, and in early stages, or limited numbers, of society, are often practically, united in the same person or persons.

112. Also, it is necessary to keep clearly in view the distinction between these two kinds of law, because the possible range of law is wider in proportion to their separation. There are many points of conduct respecting which the nation may wisely express its will by a written precept or resolve, yet not enforce it by penalty :* and the expedient degree of

[* This is the only sentence which, in revising these essays, I am now inclined to question ; but the point is one of extreme difficulty. There might be a law, for instance, of

penalty is always quite a separate consideration from the expedience of the statute; for the statute may often be better enforced by mercy than severity, and is also easier in the bearing, and less likely to be abrogated. Farther, laws of precept have reference especially to youth, and concern themselves with training; but laws of judgment to manhood, and concern themselves with remedy and reward. There is a highly curious feeling in the English mind against educational law: we think no man's liberty should be interfered with till he has done irrevocable wrong; whereas it is then just too late for the only gracious and kingly interference, which is to hinder him from doing it. Make your educational laws strict, and your criminal ones may be gentle; but, leave youth its liberty, and you will have to dig dungeons for age. And it is good for a man that he "wear the yoke in his youth:" for the reins may then be of silken thread; and with sweet chime of silver

curfew, that candles should be put out, unless for necessary service, at such and such an hour, the idea of "necessary service" being quite indefinable, and no penalty possible; yet there would be a distinct consciousness of illegal conduct in young ladies' minds who danced by candlelight till dawn.]

bells at the bridle; but, for the captivity of age, you must forge the iron fetter, and cast the passing bell.

113. Since no law can be, in a final or true sense, established, but by right, (all unjust laws involving the ultimate necessity of their own abrogation), the law-giving can only become a law-sustaining power in so far as it is Royal, or "right doing;"—in so far, that is, as it rules, not mis-rules, and orders, not dis-orders, the things submitted to it. Throned on this rock of justice, the kingly power becomes established and establishing; "θεῖος," or divine, and, therefore, it is literally true that no ruler can err, so long as he is a ruler, or ἄρχων οὐδεὶς ἁμαρτάνει τότε ὅταν ἄρχων ᾖ; perverted by careless thought, which has cost the world somewhat, into—"the king can do no wrong."

114. B. MERISTIC LAW,* or that of the tenure of property, first determines what every individual possesses by right, and secures it to him; and what he possesses by wrong,

[* Read this and the next paragraph with attention; they contain clear statements, which I cannot mend, of things most necessary.]

and deprives him of it. But it has a far higher provisory function: it determines what every man *should* possess, and puts it within his reach on due conditions; and what he should *not* possess, and puts this out of his reach, conclusively.

115. Every article of human wealth has certain conditions attached to its merited possession; when these are unobserved, possession becomes rapine. And the object of meristic law is not only to secure to every man his rightful share (the share, that is, which he has worked for, produced, or received by gift from a rightful owner), but to enforce the due conditions of possession, as far as law may conveniently reach; for instance, that land shall not be wantonly allowed to run to waste, that streams shall not be poisoned by the persons through whose properties they pass, nor air be rendered unwholesome beyond given limits. Laws of this kind exist already in rudimentary degree, but need large development: the just laws respecting the possession of works of art have not hitherto been so much as conceived, and the daily loss of national wealth, and of its use, in this

respect, is quite incalculable. And these laws need revision quite as much respecting property in national as in private hands. For instance: the public are under a vague impression that, because they have paid for the contents of the British Museum, every one has an equal right to see and to handle them. But the public have similarly paid for the contents of Woolwich arsenal; yet do not expect free access to it, or handling of its contents. The British Museum is neither a free circulating library, nor a free school: it is a place for the safe preservation, and exhibition on due occasion, of unique books, unique objects of natural history, and unique works of art; its books can no more be used by everybody than its coins can be handled, or its statues cast. There ought to be free libraries in every quarter of London, with large and complete reading-rooms attached; so also free educational museums should be open in every quarter of London, all day long, and till late at night, well lighted, well catalogued, and rich in contents both of art and natural history. But neither the British Museum nor National Gallery is a school;

they are *treasuries;* and both should be severely restricted in access and in use. Unless some order of this kind is made, and that soon, for the MSS. department of the Museum, (its superintendents have sorrowfully told me this, and repeatedly,) the best MSS. in the collection will be destroyed, irretrievably, by the careless and continual handling to which they are now subjected.

Finally, in certain conditions of a nation's progress, laws limiting accumulation of any kind of property may be found expedient.

116. C. CRITIC LAW determines questions of injury, and assigns due rewards and punishments to conduct.

Two curious economical questions arise laterally with respect to this branch of law, namely, the cost of crime, and the cost of judgment. The cost of crime is endured by nations ignorantly, that expense being nowhere stated in their budgets; the cost of judgment, patiently, (provided only it can be had pure for the money,) because the science, or perhaps we ought rather to say the art, of law, is felt to found a noble profession and discipline; so that civilized nations are usually glad that a number of persons should be supported by exercise in oratory and analysis. But it has not yet been calculated what the practical value might have been, in other directions, of the intelligence now occupied in deciding, through courses of years, what might have been decided as justly, had the date of judgment been fixed, in as many hours. Imagine one half of the funds which any great nation devotes to dispute by law, applied to the determination of physical questions in medicine, agriculture, and theoretic science; and calculate the probable results within the next ten years!

I say nothing yet of the more deadly, more lamentable loss, involved in the use of purchased, instead of personal, justice—"ἐπακτῷ παρ' ἄλλων—ἀπορίᾳ οἰκείων."

117. In order to true analysis of critic law, we must understand the real meaning of the word "injury."

We commonly understand by it, any kind of harm done by one man to another; but we do not define the idea of harm: sometimes we limit it to the harm which the sufferer is conscious of; whereas much the worst injuries are those he is *un*conscious of; and, at other times, we limit the idea to violence, or restraint; whereas much the worse forms of injury are to be accomplished by indolence, and the withdrawal of restraint.

118. "Injury" is then simply the refusal, or violation of, any man's right or claim upon his fellows: which claim, much talked of in modern times, under the term "right," is mainly resolvable into two branches: a man's claim not to be hindered from doing what he should; and his claim to be hindered from doing what he should not; these two forms of hindrance being intensified by reward, help, and fortune, or Fors, on one side, and by punishment, impediment, and even final arrest, or Mors, on the other.

119. Now, in order to a man's obtaining these two rights, it is clearly needful that the *worth* of him should be approximately known; as well as the *want* of worth, which has, unhappily, been usually the principal subject of study for critic law, careful hitherto only to mark degrees of de-merit, instead of merit;— assigning, indeed, to the *De*ficiencies (not

always, alas! even to these) just estimate, fine, or penalty; but to the *E*fficiencies, on the other side, which are by much the more interesting, as well as the only profitable part of its subject, assigning neither estimate nor aid.

120. Now, it is in this higher and perfect function of critic law, *en*abling instead of *dis*abling, that it becomes truly Kingly, instead of Draconic: (what Providence gave the great, wrathful legislator his name?): that is, it becomes the law of man and of life, instead of the law of the worm and of death—both of these laws being set in changeless poise one against another, and the enforcement of both being the eternal function of the lawgiver, and true claim of every living soul: such claim being indeed strong to be mercifully hindered, and even, if need be, abolished, when longer existence means only deeper destruction, but stronger still to be mercifully helped, and recreated, when longer existence and new creation mean nobler life. So that reward and punishment will be found to resolve themselves mainly * into help and hindrance; and

[* Mainly; not altogether. Conclusive reward of high virtue is loving and crowning, not helping; and conclusive these again will issue naturally from true recognition of deserving, and the just reverence and just wrath which follow instinctively on such recognition.

121. I say, "follow," but, in reality, they are part of the recognition. Reverence is as instinctive as anger;—both of them instant on true vision: it is sight and understanding that we have to teach, and these *are* reverence. Make a man perceive worth, and in its reflection he sees his own relative unworth, and worships thereupon inevitably, not with stiff courtesy, but rejoicingly, passionately, and, best of all, *restfully*: for the inner capacity of awe and love is infinite in man; and only in finding these, can we find peace. And the common insolences and petulances of the people, and their talk of equality, are not irreverence in them in the least, but mere blindness, stupefaction, and fog in the brains,* the first sign of punishment of deep vice is hating and crushing, not merely hindering.]

* Compare Chaucer's "villany" (clownishness).

> Full foul and chorlishe seemed she,
> And eke villanous for to be,
> And little coulde of norture
> To worship any creature.

any cleansing away of which is, that they gain some power of discerning, and some patience in submitting to, their true counsellors and governors. In the mode of such discernment consists the real "constitution" of the state, more than in the titles or offices of the discerned person; for it is no matter, save in degree of mischief, to what office a man is appointed, if he cannot fulfil it.

122. III. GOVERNMENT BY COUNCIL.

This is the determination, by living authority, of the national conduct to be observed under existing circumstances; and the modification or enlargement, abrogation or enforcement, of the code of national law according to present needs or purposes. This government is necessarily always by council, for though the authority of it may be vested in one person, that person cannot form any opinion on a matter of public interest but by (voluntarily or involuntarily) submitting himself to the influence of others.

This government is always twofold—visible and invisible.

The visible government is that which

nominally carries on the national business; determines its foreign relations, raises taxes, levies soldiers, orders war or peace, and otherwise becomes the arbiter of the national fortune. The invisible government is that exercised by all energetic and intelligent men, each in his sphere, regulating the inner will and secret ways of the people, essentially forming its character, and preparing its fate.

Visible governments are the toys of some nations, the diseases of others, the harness of some, the burdens of more, the necessity of all. Sometimes their career is quite distinct from that of the people, and to write it, as the national history, is as if one should number the accidents which befall a man's weapons and wardrobe, and call the list his biography. Nevertheless, a truly noble and wise nation necessarily has a noble and wise visible government, for its wisdom issues in that conclusively.

123. Visible governments are, in their agencies, capable of three pure forms, and of no more than three.

They are either monarchies, where the authority is vested in one person; oligarchies, when it is vested in a minority; or democracies, when vested in a majority.

But these three forms are not only, in practice, variously limited and combined, but capable of infinite difference in character and use, receiving specific names according to their variations; which names, being nowise agreed upon, nor consistently used, either in thought or writing, no man can at present tell, in speaking of any kind of government, whether he is understood; nor, in hearing, whether he understands. Thus we usually call a just government by one person a monarchy, and an unjust and cruel one, a tyranny: this might be reasonable if it had reference to the divinity of true government; but to limit the term "oligarchy" to government by a few rich people, and to call government by a few wise or noble people "aristocracy," evidently is absurd, unless it were proved that rich people never could be wise, or noble people rich; and farther absurd, because there are other distinctions in character, as well as riches or wisdom (greater purity of race, or strength of purpose, for instance), which may give the power of government to the few. So that if we had to give names to every group or kind of minority, we should have verbiage enough. But there is only one right name—"oligarchy."

124. So also the terms "republic" and "democracy"* are confused, especially in modern use; and both of them are liable to every sort of misconception. A republic means, properly, a polity in which the state, with its all, is at every man's service, and every man, with his all, at the state's service—(people are apt to lose sight of the last condition,) but its government may nevertheless be oligarchic (consular, or decemviral, for instance), or monarchic (dictatorial). But a democracy means a state in which the government rests directly with the majority of the citizens. And both these conditions have been judged only by such accidents and aspects of them as each of us has had experience of; and sometimes both have been confused with anarchy, as it is the fashion at present to talk of the "failure of republican institutions in America,"

[* I leave this paragraph, in every syllable, as it was written, during the rage of the American war; it was meant to refer, however, chiefly to the Northerns: what modifications its hot and partial terms require I will give in another place: let it stand here as it stood.]

when there has never yet been in America any such thing as an institution, but only defiance of institution; neither any such thing as a *res-publica*, but only a multitudinous *res-privata;* every man for himself. It is not republicanism which fails now in America; it is your model science of political economy, brought to its perfect practice. There you may see competition, and the "law of demand and supply" (especially in paper), in beautiful and unhindered operation.* Lust of wealth, and trust in it; vulgar faith in magnitude and multitude, instead of nobleness; besides that faith natural to backwoods-men—"lucum ligna,"†—perpetual self-contemplation issuing in passionate vanity; total ignorance of the finer and higher arts, and of all that they teach and bestow; and the discontent of energetic minds unoccupied, frantic with hope of

---

* Supply and demand! Alas! for what noble work was there ever any audible "demand" in that poor sense (Past and Present)? Nay, the demand is not loud, even for ignoble work. *See* "Average Earnings of Betty Taylor," in *Times* of 4th February of this year [1863]: "Worked from Monday morning at 8 A.M. to Friday night at 5.30 P.M. for 1s 5½d."—*Laissez faire.* [This kind of slavery finds no Abolitionists that I hear of.]

[† "That the sacred grove is nothing but logs."]

uncomprehended change, and progress they know not whither;*—these are the things that have "failed" in America; and yet not altogether failed—it is not collapse, but collision; the greatest railroad accident on record, with fire caught from the furnace, and Catiline's quenching "non aquâ, sed ruinâ."† But I see not, in any of our talk of them, justice enough done to their erratic strength of purpose, nor any estimate taken of the strength of endurance of domestic sorrow, in what their women and children suppose a righteous cause. And out

* Ames, by report of Waldo Emerson, says "that a monarchy is a merchantman, which sails well, but will sometimes strike on a rock, and go to the bottom; whilst a republic is a raft, which would never sink, but then your feet are always in the water." Yes, that is comfortable; and though your raft cannot sink (being too worthless for that), it may go to pieces, I suppose, when the four winds (your only pilots) steer competitively from its four corners, and carry it, ὡς ὀπωρινὸς Βορέης φορέησιν ἀκάνθας, and then more than your feet will be in the water.

[† "Not with water, but with ruin." The worst ruin being that which the Americans chiefly boast of. They sent all their best and honestest youths, Harvard University men and the like, to that accursed war; got them nearly all shot; wrote pretty biographies (to the ages of 17, 18, 19) and epitaphs for them; and so, having washed all the salt out of the nation in blood, left themselves to putrefaction, and the morality of New York.]

of that endurance and suffering, its own fruit will be born with time; [*not* abolition of slavery, however. See § 130] and Carlyle's prophecy of them (June, 1850), as it has now come true in the first clause, will, in the last:—

"America, too, will find that caucuses, division-lists, stump-oratory, and speeches to Buncombe will not carry men to the immortal gods; that the Washington Congress, and constitutional battle of Kilkenny cats is there, as here, naught for such objects; quite incompetent for such; and, in fine, that said sublime constitutional arrangement will require to be (with terrible throes, and travail such as few expect yet) remodelled, abridged, extended, suppressed, torn asunder, put together again; —not without heroic labour and effort, quite other than that of the stump-orator and the revival preacher, one day."

125.* Understand, then, once for all, that no form of government, provided it be a government at all, is, as such, to be either condemned or praised, or contested for in anywise, but by fools. But all forms of government are good just so far as they attain this one vital

[* This paragraph contains the gist of all that precede.]

necessity of policy—*that the wise and kind, few or many, shall govern the unwise and unkind;* and they are evil so far as they miss of this, or reverse it. Nor does the form, in any case, signify one whit, but its *firmness*, and adaptation to the need; for if there be many foolish persons in a state, and few wise, then it is good that the few govern; and if there be many wise, and few foolish, then it is good that the many govern; and if many be wise, yet one wiser, then it is good that one should govern; and so on. Thus, we may have "the ant's republic, and the realm of bees," both good in their kind; one for groping, and the other for building; and nobler still, for flying; —the Ducal monarchy * of those

> Intelligent of seasons, that set forth
> The aery caravan, high over seas.

126. Nor need we want examples, among the inferior creatures, of dissoluteness, as well

[* Whenever you are puzzled by any apparently mistaken use of words in these essays, take your dictionary, remembering I had to fix terms, as well as principles. A Duke is a "dux" or "leader;" the flying wedge of cranes is under a "ducal monarch"—a very different personage from a queen-bee. The Venetians, with a beautiful instinct, gave the name to their King of the Sea.]

as resoluteness, in government. I once saw democracy finely illustrated by the beetles of North Switzerland, who by universal suffrage, and elytric acclamation, one May twilight, carried it, that they would fly over the Lake of Zug; and flew *short*, to the great disfigurement of the Lake of Zug,—Κανθάρου λιμήν—over some leagues square, and to the close of the cockchafer democracy for that year. Then, for tyranny, the old fable of the frogs and the stork finely touches one form of it; but truth will image it more closely than fable, for tyranny is not complete when it is only over the idle, but when it is over the laborious and the blind. This description of pelicans and climbing perch, which I find quoted in one of our popular natural histories, out of Sir Emerson Tennant's *Ceylon*, comes as near as may be to the true image of the thing:—

"Heavy rains came on, and as we stood on the high ground, we observed a pelican on the margin of the shallow pool gorging himself; our people went towards him, and raised a cry of 'Fish, fish!' We hurried down, and found numbers of fish struggling upward through the grass, in the rills formed by the trickling of the rain. There was scarcely water to cover them, but nevertheless they made rapid progress up the bank, on which our followers collected about two baskets of them. They were forcing their way up the knoll, and had they not been interrupted, first by the pelican, and afterwards by ourselves, they would in a few minutes have gained the highest point, and descended on the other side into a pool which formed another portion of the tank. In going this distance, however, they must have used muscular exertion enough to have taken them half a mile on level ground; for at these places all the cattle and wild animals of the neighbourhood had latterly come to drink, so that the surface was everywhere indented with footmarks, in addition to the cracks in the surrounding baked mud, into which the fish tumbled in their progress. In those holes, which were deep, and the sides perpendicular, they remained to die, and were carried off by kites and crows." *

[* This is a perfect picture of the French under the tyrannies of their Pelican Kings, before the Revolution. But they must find other than Pelican Kings—or rather, Pelican Kings of the Divine brood, that feed their children, and with their best blood.]

127. But whether governments be bad or good, one general disadvantage seems to attach to them in modern times—that they are all *costly*.* This, however, is not essentially the fault of the governments. If nations choose to play at war, they will always find their governments willing to lead the game, and soon coming under that term of Aristophanes, "κάπηλοι ἀσπίδων," "shield-sellers." And when (πῆμ' ἐπὶ πήματι †) the shields take the form of iron ships, with apparatus "for defence against liquid fire,"—as I see by latest accounts they are now arranging the decks in English dockyards—they become costly biers enough for the grey convoy of chief-mourner waves, wreathed with funereal foam, to bear back the dead upon; the massy shoulders of those corpse-bearers being intended for quite other work, and to bear the living, and food for the living, if we would let them.

128. Nor have we the least right to complain

[* Read carefully, from this point; because here begins the statement of things requiring to be done, which I am now re-trying to make definite in *Fors Clavigera*.]

[† "Evil on the top of Evil." Delphic oracle, meaning iron on the anvil.]

of our governments being expensive, so long as we set the government *to do precisely the work which brings no return.* If our present doctrines of political economy be just, let us trust them to the utmost; take that war business out of the government's hands, and test therein the principles of supply and demand. Let our future sieges of Sebastopol be done by contract—no capture, no pay—(I admit that things might sometimes go better so); and let us sell the commands of our prospective battles, with our vicarages, to the lowest bidder; so may we have cheap victories, and divinity. On the other hand, if we have so much suspicion of our science that we dare not trust it on military or spiritual business, would it not be but reasonable to try whether some authoritative handling may not prosper in matters utilitarian? If we were to set our governments to do useful things instead of mischievous, possibly even the apparatus itself might in time come to be less costly. The machine, applied to the building of the house, might perhaps pay, when it seems not to pay, applied to pulling it down. If we made in our dockyards ships to carry timber and coals, instead of cannon, and with provision for the brightening of domestic solid culinary fire, instead of for the scattering of liquid hostile fire, it might have some effect on the taxes. Or suppose that we tried the experiment on land instead of water carriage; already the government, not unapproved, carries letters and parcels for us; larger packages may in time follow;—even general merchandise—why not, at last, ourselves? Had the money spent in local mistakes and vain private litigation, on the railroads of England, been laid out, instead, under proper government restraint, on really useful railroad work, and had no absurd expense been incurred in ornamenting stations, we might already have had,—what ultimately it will be found we must have,—quadruple rails, two for passengers, and two for traffic, on every great line; and we might have been carried in swift safety, and watched and warded by well-paid pointsmen, for half the present fares. [For, of course, a railroad company is merely an association of turnpike-keepers, who make the tolls as high as they can, not to mend the roads with, but to pocket. The public will in time discover this, and do away with turnpikes on railroads, as on all other public-ways.]

129. Suppose it should thus turn out, finally, that a true government set to true work, instead of being a costly engine, was a paying one? that your government, rightly organized, instead of itself subsisting by an income-tax, would produce its subjects some subsistence in the shape of an income dividend?—police, and judges duly paid besides, only with less work than the state at present provides for them.

A true government set to true work!—Not easily to be imagined, still less obtained; but not beyond human hope or ingenuity. Only you will have to alter your election systems somewhat, first. Not by universal suffrage, nor by votes purchaseable with beer, is such government to be had. That is to say, not by universal *equal* suffrage. Every man upwards of twenty, who had been convicted of no legal crime, should have his say in this matter; but afterwards a louder voice, as he grows older, and approves himself wiser. If he has one vote at twenty, he should have two at thirty, four at forty, ten at fifty. For every single vote which he has with an income of a hundred a year, he should have ten with an income of a thousand, (provided you first see to it that wealth is, as nature intended it to be, the reward of sagacity and industry—not of good luck in a scramble or a lottery). For every single vote which he had as subordinate in any business, he should have two when he became a master; and every office and authority nationally bestowed, implying trustworthiness and intellect, should have its known proportional number of votes attached to it. But into the detail and working of a true system in these matters we cannot now enter; we are concerned as yet with definitions only, and statements of first principles, which will be established now sufficiently for our purposes when we have examined the nature of that form of government last on the list in § 105,—the purely "Magistral," exciting at present its full share of public notice, under its ambiguous title of "slavery."

130. I have not, however, been able to ascertain in definite terms, from the declaimers against slavery, what they understand by it. If they mean only the imprisonment or

compulsion of one person by another, such imprisonment or compulsion being in many cases highly expedient, slavery, so defined, would be no evil in itself, but only in its abuse; that is, when men are slaves, who should not be, or masters, who should not be, or even the fittest characters for either state, placed in it under conditions which should not be. It is not, for instance, a necessary condition of slavery, nor a desirable one, that parents should be separated from children, or husbands from wives; but the institution of war, against which people declaim with less violence, effects such separations,—not unfrequently in a very permanent manner. To press a sailor, seize a white youth by conscription for a soldier, or carry off a black one for a labourer, may all be right acts or all wrong ones, according to needs and circumstances. It is wrong to scourge a man unnecessarily. So it is to shoot him. Both must be done on occasion; and it is better and kinder to flog a man to his work, than to leave him idle till he robs, and flog him afterwards. The essential thing for all creatures is to be made to do right; how they are made to do it

—by pleasant promises, or hard necessities, pathetic oratory, or the whip—is comparatively immaterial.* To be deceived is perhaps as incompatible with human dignity as to be whipped; and I suspect the last method to be not the worst, for the help of many individuals. The Jewish nation throve under it, in the hand of a monarch reputed not unwise; it is only the change of whip for scorpion which is inexpedient; and that change is as likely to come to pass on the side of license as of law. For the true scorpion whips are those of the nation's pleasant vices, which are to it as St. John's locusts—crown on the head, ravin in the mouth, and sting in the tail. If it will not bear the rule of Athena and Apollo, who shepherd without smiting (οὐ πληγῇ νέμοντες), Athena at last calls no more in the corners of the streets; and then follows the rule of Tisiphone, who smites without shepherding.

131. If, however, by slavery, instead of absolute compulsion, is meant *the purchase, by money, of the right of compulsion,* such purchase

[* Permit me to enforce and reinforce this statement, with all earnestness. It is the sum of what needs most to be understood, in the matter of education.]

is necessarily made whenever a portion of any territory is transferred, for money, from one monarch to another: which has happened frequently enough in history, without its being supposed that the inhabitants of the districts so transferred became therefore slaves. In this, as in the former case, the dispute seems about the fashion of the thing, rather than the fact of it. There are two rocks in mid-sea, on each of which, neglected equally by instructive and commercial powers, a handful of inhabitants live as they may. Two merchants bid for the two properties, but not in the same terms. One bids for the people, buys *them*, and sets them to work, under pain of scourge; the other bids for the rock, buys *it*, and throws the inhabitants into the sea. The former is the American, the latter the English method, of slavery; much is to be said for, and something against, both, which I hope to say in due time and place.*

132. If, however, slavery mean not merely the purchase of the right of compulsion, but *the purchase of the body and soul of the creature*

[* A pregnant paragraph, meant against English and Scotch landlords who drive their people off the land.]

itself for money, it is not, I think, among the black races that purchases of this kind are most extensively made, or that separate souls of a fine make fetch the highest price. This branch of the inquiry we shall have occasion also to follow out at some length, for in the worst instances of the selling of souls, we are apt to get, when we ask if the sale is valid, only Pyrrhon's answer*—" None can know."

133. The fact is that slavery is not a political institution at all, *but an inherent, natural, and eternal inheritance* of a large portion of the human race—to whom, the more you give of their own free will, the more slaves they will make themselves. In common parlance, we idly confuse captivity with slavery, and are always thinking of the difference between pine-trunks (Ariel in the pine), and cowslip-bells ("in the cowslip-bell I lie"), or between carrying wood and drinking (Caliban's slavery and freedom), instead of noting the far more serious differences between Ariel and Caliban themselves, and the means by which, practically, that difference may be brought about or diminished.

[* In Lucian's dialogue, " The sale of lives."]

134.* Plato's slave, in the *Polity*, who, well dressed and washed, aspires to the hand of his master's daughter, corresponds curiously to Caliban attacking Prospero's cell; and there is an undercurrent of meaning throughout, in the *Tempest* as well as in the *Merchant of Venice;* referring in this case to government, as in that to commerce. Miranda †

[* I raise this analysis of the *Tempest* into my text; but it is nothing but a hurried note, which I may never have time to expand. I have retouched it here and there a little, however.]

† Of Shakspeare's names I will afterwards speak at more length: they are curiously—often barbarously—much by Providence,—but assuredly not without Shakspeare's cunning purpose—mixed out of the various traditions he confusedly adopted, and languages which he imperfectly knew. Three of the clearest in meaning have been already noticed, Desdemona, "δυσδαιμονία," "miserable fortune," is also plain enough. Othello is, I believe, "the careful;" all the calamity of the tragedy arising from the single flaw and error in his magnificently collected strength. Ophelia, "serviceableness," the true lost wife of Hamlet, is marked as having a Greek name by that of her brother, Laertes; and its signification is once exquisitely alluded to in that brother's last word of her, where her gentle preciousness is opposed to the uselessness of the churlish clergy—"A *ministering* angel shall my sister be, when thou liest howling." Hamlet is, I believe, connected in some way with "homely," the entire event of the tragedy turning on betrayal of home duty. Hermione (ἕρμα), "pillar-like" (ἢ εἶδος ἔχε χρυσῆς 'Αφροδίτης). Titania (τιτήνη), "the queen;"

("the wonderful," so addressed first by Ferdinand, "Oh, you wonder!") corresponds to Homer's Arete: Ariel and Caliban are respectively the spirits of faithful and imaginative labour, opposed to rebellious, hurtful, and slavish labour. Prospero ("for hope"), a true governor, is opposed to Sycorax, the mother of slavery, her name "Swine-raven" indicating at once brutality and deathfulness; hence the line—

"As wicked dew as e'er my mother brushed with *raven's feather*,"—etc.

For all these dreams of Shakspeare, as those of true and strong men must be, are "$\phi\alpha\nu\tau\acute{\alpha}\sigma$-$\mu\alpha\tau\alpha$ $\theta\epsilon\hat{\iota}\alpha$, $\kappa\alpha\grave{\iota}$ $\sigma\kappa\iota\alpha\grave{\iota}$ $\tau\hat{\omega}\nu$ $\check{o}\nu\tau\omega\nu$"—divine phantasms, and shadows of things that are. We hardly tell our children, willingly, a fable with no purport in it; yet we think God sends his best messengers only to sing fairy tales to

Benedict and Beatrice, "blessed and blessing;" Valentine and Proteus, enduring (or strong), (valens), and changeful. Iago and Iachimo have evidently the same root—probably the Spanish Iago, Jacob, "the supplanter." Leonatus, and other such names, are interpreted, or played with, in the plays themselves. For the interpretation of Sycorax, and reference to her raven's feather, I am indebted to Mr. John R. Wise.

us, fond and empty. The *Tempest* is just like a grotesque in a rich missal, "clasped where paynims pray." Ariel is the spirit of generous and free-hearted service, in early stages of human society oppressed by ignorance and wild tyranny: venting groans as fast as millwheels strike; in shipwreck of states, dreadful; so that "all but mariners plunge in the brine, and quit the vessel, then all afire with *me*," yet having in itself the will and sweetness of truest peace, whence that is especially called "Ariel's" song, "Come unto these yellow sands, and there, *take hands*, courtesied when you have, and kissed, the wild waves whist:" (mind, it is "cortesia," not "curtsey,") and read "quiet" for "whist," if you want the full sense. Then you may indeed foot it featly, and sweet spirits bear the burden for you—with watch in the night, and call in early morning. The *vis viva* in elemental transformation follows—"Full fathom five thy father lies, of his bones are coral made." Then, giving rest *after* labour, it "fetches dew from the still vext Bermoöthes, and, with a charm joined to their suffered labour, leaves men asleep." Snatching away the feast of the cruel, it seems to them as a harpy; followed by the utterly vile, who cannot see it in any shape, but to whom it is the picture of nobody, it still gives shrill harmony to their false and mocking catch, "Thought is free;" but leads them into briars and foul places, and at last hollas the hounds upon them. Minister of fate against the great criminal, it joins itself with the "incensed seas and shores"—the sword that layeth at it cannot hold, and may "with bemocked-at stabs as soon kill the still-closing waters, as diminish one dowle that is in its plume." As the guide and aid of true love, it is always called by Prospero "fine" (the French "fine," not the English), or "delicate"—another long note would be needed to explain all the meaning in this word. Lastly, its work done, and war, it resolves itself into the elements. The intense significance of the last song, "Where the bee sucks," I will examine in its due place.

The types of slavery in Caliban are more palpable, and need not be dwelt on now: though I will notice them also, severally, in their proper places;—the heart of his slavery is in his worship: "That's a brave god, and bears celestial—liquor." But, in illustration of the sense in which the Latin "benignus" and "malignus" are to be coupled with Eleutheria and Douleia, note that Caliban's torment is always the physical reflection of his own nature—"cramps" and "side stitches that shall pen thy breath up; thou shalt be pinched, as thick as honeycombs:" the whole nature of slavery being one cramp and cretinous contraction. Fancy this of Ariel! You may fetter him, but you set no mark on him; you may put him to hard work and far journey, but you cannot give him a cramp.

135. I should dwell, even in these prefatory papers, at more length on this subject of slavery, had not all I would say been said already, in vain, (not, as I hope, ultimately in vain,) by Carlyle, in the first of the *Latter-day Pamphlets*, which I commend to the reader's gravest reading; together with that as much neglected, and still more immediately needed, on model prisons, and with the great chapter on "Permanence" (fifth of the last section of "Past and Present"), which sums what is known, and foreshadows, or rather forelights, all that is to be learned of National

Discipline. I have only here farther to examine the nature of one world-wide and everlasting form of slavery, wholesome in use, as deadly in abuse;—the service of the rich by the poor.

CHAPTER VI.

MASTERSHIP

136. As in all previous discussions of our subject, we must study the relation of the commanding rich to the obeying poor in its simplest elements, in order to reach its first principles.

The simplest state of it, then, is this:* a wise and provident person works much, consumes little, and lays by a store; an improvident person works little, consumes all his produce, and lays by no store. Accident interrupts the daily work, or renders it less productive; the idle person must then starve or be supported by the provident one, who, having him thus at his mercy, may either

---

* In the present general examination I concede so much to ordinary economists as to ignore all *innocent* poverty. I adapt my reasoning, for once, to the modern English practical mind, by assuming poverty to be always criminal; the conceivable exceptions we will examine afterwards.

refuse to maintain him altogether, or, which will evidently be more to his own interest, say to him, "I will maintain you, indeed, but you shall now work hard, instead of indolently, and instead of being allowed to lay by what you save, as you might have done, had you remained independent, *I* will take all the surplus. You would not lay it up for yourself; it is wholly your own fault that has thrown you into my power, and I will force you to work, or starve; yet you shall have no profit of your work, only your daily bread for it; [and competition shall determine how much of that *]." This mode of treatment has now become so universal that it is supposed to be the only natural—nay, the only possible one; and the market wages are calmly defined by economists as "the sum which will maintain the labourer."

137. The power of the provident person to do this is only checked by the correlative power of some neighbour of similarly frugal

[* I have no terms of English, and can find none in Greek nor Latin, nor in any other strong language known to me, contemptuous enough to attack the bestial idiotism of the modern theory that wages are to be measured by competition.]

habits, who says to the labourer—" I will give you a little more than this other provident person : come and work for me."

The power of the provident over the improvident depends thus, primarily, on their relative numbers; secondarily, on the modes of agreement of the adverse parties with each other. The accidental level of wages is a variable function of the number of provident and idle persons in the world, of the enmity between them as classes, and of the agreement between those of the same class. *It depends, from beginning to end, on moral conditions.*

138. Supposing the rich to be entirely selfish, *it is always for their interest that the poor should be as numerous as they can employ, and restrain.* For, granting that the entire population is no larger than the ground can easily maintain—that the classes are stringently divided—and that there is sense or strength of hand enough with the rich to secure obedience; then, if nine-tenths of a nation are poor, the remaining tenth have the service of nine persons each;[*]

---

[*] I say nothing yet of the quality of the servants, which, nevertheless, is the gist of the business. Will you have Paul

but, if eight-tenths are poor, only of four each; if seven-tenths are poor, of two and a third each; if six-tenths are poor, of one and a half each; and if five-tenths are poor, of only one each. But, practically, if the rich strive always to obtain more power over the poor, instead of to raise them—and if, on the other hand, the poor become continually more vicious and numerous, through neglect and oppression, —though the *range* of the power of the rich increases, its *tenure* becomes less secure; until, at last, the measure of iniquity being full, revolution, civil war, or the subjection of the state to a healthier or stronger one, closes the moral corruption, and industrial disease.*

139. It is rarely, however, that things come to this extremity. Kind persons among the rich, and wise among the poor, modify the connexion of the classes; the efforts made to

---

Veronese to paint your ceiling, or the plumber from over the way? Both will work for the same money; Paul, if anything, a little the cheaper of the two, if you keep him in good humour; only you have to discern him first, which will need eyes.

[* I have not altered a syllable in these three paragraphs, 137, 138, 139, on revision: but have much italicised: the principles stated being as vital, as they are little known.]

raise and relieve on the one side, and the success of honest toil on the other, bind and blend the orders of society into the confused tissue of half-felt obligation, sullenly-rendered obedience, and variously-directed, or mis-directed, toil, which form the warp of daily life. But this great law rules all the wild design : that success (while society is guided by laws of competition) *signifies always so much victory over your neighbour* as to obtain the direction of his work, and to take the profits of it. *This is the real source of all great riches.* No man can become largely rich by his personal toil.* The work of his own hands, wisely directed, will indeed always maintain himself and his family, and make fitting provision for his age. *But it is only by the discovery of some method of taxing the labour of others that he can become opulent.* Every increase of his capital enables him to extend this taxation more widely; that is, to invest larger funds in the maintenance of labourers,—to direct, accordingly, vaster and

---

* By his art he may ; but only when its produce, or the sight or hearing of it, becomes a subject of dispute, so as to enable the artist to tax the labour of multitudes highly, in exchange for his own.

yet vaster masses of labour, and to appropriate its profits.

140. There is much confusion of idea on the subject of this appropriation. It is, of course, the interest of the employer to disguise it from the persons employed; and, for his own comfort and complacency, he often desires no less to disguise it from himself. And it is matter of much doubt with me, how far the foul and foolish arguments used habitually on this subject are indeed the honest expression of foul and foolish convictions;—or rather (as I am sometimes forced to conclude from the irritation with which they are advanced) are resolutely dishonest, wilful, and malicious sophisms, arranged so as to mask, to the last moment, the real laws of economy, and future duties of men. By taking a simple example, and working it thoroughly out, the subject may be rescued from all but such determined misrepresentation.

141. Let us imagine a society of peasants, living on a river-shore, exposed to destructive inundation at somewhat extended intervals; and that each peasant possesses of this good, but imperilled, ground, more than he needs to

cultivate for immediate subsistence. We will assume farther (and with too great probability of justice), that the greater part of them indolently keep in tillage just as much land as supplies them with daily food;—that they leave their children idle, and take no precautions against the rise of the stream. But one of them, (we will say but one, for the sake of greater clearness) cultivates carefully *all* the ground of his estate; makes his children work hard and healthily; uses his spare time and theirs in building a rampart against the river; and, at the end of some years, has in his storehouses large reserves of food and clothing,—in his stables a well-tended breed of cattle, and around his fields a wedge of wall against flood.

The torrent rises at last—sweeps away the harvests, and half the cottages of the careless peasants, and leaves them destitute. They naturally come for help to the provident one, whose fields are unwasted, and whose granaries are full. He has the right to refuse it to them: no one disputes this right.* But he will

[* Observe this; the legal right to keep what you have worked for, and use it as you please, is the corner-stone of all economy: compare the end of Chap. II.]

probably *not* refuse it; it is not his interest to do so, even were he entirely selfish and cruel. The only question with him will be on what terms his aid is to be granted.

142. Clearly, not on terms of mere charity. To maintain his neighbours in idleness would be not only his ruin, but theirs. He will require work from them, in exchange for their maintenance; and, whether in kindness or cruelty, all the work they can give. Not now the three or four hours they were wont to spend on their own land, but the eight or ten hours they ought to have spent.* But how will he apply this labour? The men are now his slaves;—nothing less, and nothing more. On pain of starvation, he can force them to work in the manner, and to the end, he chooses. And it is by his wisdom in this choice that the worthiness of his mastership is proved, or its unworthiness. Evidently, he must first set them to bank out the water in some temporary way, and to get their ground cleansed and resown; else, in any case, their continued maintenance will be impossible. That done,

[* I should now put the time of necessary labour rather under than over the third of the day.]

and while he has still to feed them, suppose he makes them raise a secure rampart for their own ground against all future flood, and rebuild their houses in safer places, with the best material they can find; being allowed time out of their working hours to fetch such material from a distance. And for the food and clothing advanced, he takes security in land that as much shall be returned at a convenient period.

143. We may conceive this security to be redeemed, and the debt paid at the end of a few years. The prudent peasant has sustained no loss; *but is no richer than he was, and has had all his trouble for nothing.* But he has enriched his neighbours materially; bettered their houses, secured their land, and rendered them, in worldly matters, equal to himself. In all rational and final sense, he has been throughout their true Lord and King.

144. We will next trace his probable line of conduct, presuming his object to be exclusively the increase of his own fortune. After roughly recovering and cleansing the ground, he allows the ruined peasantry only to build huts upon it, such as he thinks protective enough from the weather to keep them in

working health. The rest of their time he occupies, first in pulling down, and rebuilding on a magnificent scale, his own house, and in adding large dependencies to it. This done, in exchange for his continued supply of corn, he buys as much of his neighbours' land as he thinks he can superintend the management of; and makes the former owners securely embank and protect the ceded portion. By this arrangement, he leaves to a certain number of the peasantry only as much ground as will just maintain them in their existing numbers; as the population increases, he takes the extra hands, who cannot be maintained on the narrowed estates, for his own servants; employs some to cultivate the ground he has bought, giving them of its produce merely enough for subsistence; with the surplus, which, under his energetic and careful superintendence, will be large, he maintains a train of servants for state, and a body of workmen, whom he educates in ornamental arts. He now can splendidly decorate his house, lay out its grounds magnificently, and richly supply his table, and that of his household and retinue. And thus, without any abuse of right, we should find established all the phenomena of poverty and riches, which (it is supposed necessarily) accompany modern civilization. In one part of the district, we should have unhealthy land, miserable dwellings, and half-starved poor; in another, a well-ordered estate, well-fed servants, and refined conditions of highly-educated and luxurious life.

145. I have put the two cases in simplicity, and to some extremity. But though in more complex and qualified operation, all the relations of society are but the expansion of these two typical sequences of conduct and result. I do not say, observe, that the first procedure is entirely recommendable; or even entirely right; still less, that the second is wholly wrong. Servants, and artists, and splendour of habitation and retinue, have all their use, propriety, and office. But I am determined that the reader shall understand clearly what they cost; and see that the condition of having them is the subjection to us of a certain number of imprudent or unfortunate persons (or, it may be, more fortunate than their masters), over whose destinies we exercise a boundless control. "Riches" mean

eternally and essentially this; and God send at last a time when those words of our best-reputed economist shall be true, and we *shall* indeed "all know what it is to be rich;"* that it is to be slave-master over farthest earth, and over all ways and thoughts of men. Every operative you employ is your true servant: distant or near, subject to your immediate orders, or ministering to your widely-communicated caprice,—for the pay he stipulates, or the price he tempts,—all are alike under this great dominion of the gold. The milliner who makes the dress is as much a servant (more so, in that she uses more intelligence in the service) as the maid who puts it on; the carpenter who smooths the door, as the footman who opens it; the tradesmen who supply the table, as the labourers and sailors who supply the tradesmen. Why speak of these lower services? Painters and singers (whether of note or rhyme), jesters and story-tellers, moralists, historians, priests,—so far as these, in any degree, paint, or sing, or tell their tale, or charm their charm, or "perform" their rite, *for pay*,—in so far, they are all slaves; abject

[* See Preface to *Unto this Last*.]

utterly, if the service be for pay only; abject less and less in proportion to the degrees of love and of wisdom which enter into their duty, or *can* enter into it, according as their function is to do the bidding and the work of a manly people;—or to amuse, tempt, and deceive, a childish one.

146. There is always, in such amusement and temptation, to a certain extent, a government of the rich by the poor, as of the poor by the rich; but the latter is the prevailing and necessary one, and it consists, when it is honourable, in the collection of the profits of labour from those who would have misused them, and the administration of those profits for the service either of the same persons in future, or of others; and when it is dishonourable, as is more frequently the case in modern times, it consists in the collection of the profits of labour from those who would have rightly used them, and their appropriation to the service of the collector himself.

147. The examination of these various modes of collection and use of riches will form the third branch of our future inquiries; but the key to the whole subject lies in the clear

understanding of the difference between selfish and unselfish expenditure. It is not easy, by any course of reasoning, to enforce this on the generally unwilling hearer; yet the definition of unselfish expenditure is brief and simple. It is expenditure which, if you are a capitalist, does not pay *you*, but pays somebody else; and if you are a consumer, does not please *you*, but pleases somebody else. Take one special instance, in further illustration of the general type given above. I did not invent that type, but spoke of a real river, and of real peasantry, the languid and sickly race which inhabits, or haunts—for they are often more like spectres than living men—the thorny desolation of the banks of the Arve in Savoy. Some years ago, a society, formed at Geneva, offered to embank the river for the ground which would have been recovered by the operation; but the offer was refused by the (then Sardinian) government. The capitalists saw that this expenditure would have "paid" if the ground saved from the river was to be theirs. But if, when the offer that had this aspect of profit was refused, they had nevertheless persisted in the plan, and merely taking security for the return of their outlay, lent the funds for the work, and thus saved a whole race of human souls from perishing in a pestiferous fen (as, I presume, some among them would, at personal risk, have dragged any one drowning creature out of the current of the stream, and not expected payment therefor), such expenditure would have precisely corresponded to the use of his power made, in the first instance, by our supposed richer peasant—it would have been the king's, of grace, instead of the usurer's, for gain.

148. "Impossible, absurd, Utopian!" exclaim nine-tenths of the few readers whom these words may find.

No, good reader, *this* is not Utopian: but I will tell you what would have seemed, if we had not seen it, Utopian on the side of evil instead of good; that ever men should have come to value their money so much more than their lives, that if you call upon them to become soldiers, and take chance of a bullet through their heart, and of wife and children being left desolate, for their pride's sake, they will do it gaily, without thinking twice; but if you ask them, for their country's sake, to spend a hundred pounds without security of getting back a hundred-and-five,* they will laugh in your face.

149. Not but that also this game of life-giving and taking is, in the end, somewhat more costly than other forms of play might be. Rifle practice is, indeed, a not unhealthy pastime, and a feather on the top of the head is a pleasing appendage; but while learning the stops and fingering of the sweet instrument,

---

* I have not hitherto touched on the subject of interest of money; it is too complex, and must be reserved for its proper place in the body of the work. The definition of interest (apart from compensation for risk) is, "the exponent of the comfort of accomplished labour, separated from its power;" the power being what is lent: and the French economists who have maintained the entire illegality of interest are wrong; yet by no means so curiously or wildly wrong as the English and French ones opposed to them, whose opinions have been collected by Dr. Whewell at page 41 of his *Lectures;* it never seeming to occur to the mind of the compiler, any more than to the writers whom he quotes, that it is quite possible, and even (according to Jewish proverb) prudent, for men to hoard as ants and mice do, for use, not usury; and lay by something for winter nights, in the expectation of rather sharing than lending the scrapings. My Savoyard squirrels would pass a pleasant time of it under the snow-laden pine-branches, if they always declined to economize because no one would pay them interest on nuts.

[I leave this note as it stood: but, as I have above stated, should now side wholly with the French economists spoken of, in asserting the absolute illegality of interest.]

does no one ever calculate the cost of an overture? What melody does Tityrus meditate on his tenderly spiral pipe? The leaden seed of it, broad-cast, true conical "Dents de Lion" seed—needing less allowance for the wind than is usual with that kind of herb—what crop are you likely to have of it? Suppose, instead of this volunteer marching and counter-marching, you were to do a little volunteer ploughing and counter-ploughing? It is more difficult to do it straight: the dust of the earth, so disturbed, is more grateful than for merely rhythmic footsteps. Golden cups, also, given for good ploughing, would be more suitable in colour: (ruby glass, for the wine which "giveth his colour" on the ground, might be fitter for the rifle prize in ladies' hands). Or, conceive a little volunteer exercise with the spade, other than such as is needed for moat and breastwork, or even for the burial of the fruit of the laden avena-seed, subject to the shrill Lemures' criticism—

Wer hat das Haus so schlecht gebeaut?

If you were to embank Lincolnshire more stoutly against the sea? or strip the peat of

Solway, or plant Plinlimmon moors with larch—then, in due season, some amateur reaping and threshing?

"Nay, we reap and thresh by steam, in these advanced days."

I know it, my wise and economical friends. The stout arms God gave you to win your bread by, you would fain shoot your neighbours, and God's sweet singers with;* then

---

* Compare Chaucer's feeling respecting birds (from Canace's falcon, to the nightingale, singing, "Domine, labia—" to the Lord of Love) with the usual modern British sentiments on this subject. Or even Cowley's:—

> "What prince's choir of music can excel
> That which within this shade does dwell,
> To which we nothing pay, or give,
> They, like all other poets, live
> Without reward, or thanks for their obliging pains!
> 'Tis well if they become not prey."

Yes; it is better than well; particularly since the seed sown by the wayside has been protected by the peculiar appropriation of part of the church-rates in our country parishes. See the remonstrance from a "Country Parson," in *The Times* of June 4th (or 5th; the letter is dated June 3rd), 1862:—"I have heard at a vestry meeting a good deal of higgling over a few shillings' outlay in cleaning the church; but I have never heard any dissatisfaction expressed on account of that part of the rate which is invested in 50 or 100 dozens of birds' heads."

[If we could trace the innermost of all causes of modern

you invoke the fiends to your farm-service; and—

> When young and old come forth to play
> On a sulphurous holiday,
> Tell how the darkling goblin sweat
> (His feast of cinders duly set),
> And, belching night, where breathed the morn,
> His shadowy flail hath threshed the corn
> That ten day-labourers could not end.

150. Going back to the matter in hand we will press the example closer. On a green knoll above that plain of the Arve, between Cluse and Bonneville, there was, in the year 1860, a cottage, inhabited by a well-doing family—man and wife, three children, and the grandmother. I call it a cottage, but in truth, it was a large chimney on the ground, wide at the bottom, so that the family might live round the fire; lighted by one small broken window, and entered by an unclosing door. The family, I say, was "well-doing;" at least, it was hopeful and cheerful; the wife healthy, the children, for Savoyards,

war, I believe it would be found, not in the avarice nor ambition of nations, but in the mere idleness of the upper classes. They have nothing to do but to teach the peasantry to kill each other.]

pretty and active, but the husband threatened with decline, from exposure under the cliffs of the Mont Vergi by day, and to draughts between every plank of his chimney in the frosty nights.

"Why could he not plaster the chinks?" asks the practical reader. For the same reason that your child cannot wash its face and hands till you have washed them many a day for it, and will not wash them when it can, till you force it.

151. I passed this cottage often in my walks, had its window and door mended; sometimes mended also a little the meal of sour bread and broth, and generally got kind greeting and smile from the face of young or old; which greeting, this year, narrowed itself into the half-recognising stare of the elder child, and the old woman's tears; for the father and mother were both dead,—one of sickness, the other of sorrow. It happened that I passed not alone, but with a companion, a practised English joiner, who, while these people were dying of cold, had been employed from six in the morning to six in the evening, for two months, in fitting, without nails, the panels

of a single door in a large house in London. Three days of his work taken, at the right time, from fastening the oak panels with useless precision, and applied to fasten the larch timbers with decent strength, would have saved these Savoyards' lives. *He* would have been maintained equally; (I suppose him equally paid for his work by the owner of the greater house, only the work not consumed selfishly on his own walls;) and the two peasants, and eventually, probably their children, saved.

152. There are, therefore,—let me finally enforce, and leave with the reader, this broad conclusion,—three things to be considered in employing any poor person. It is not enough to give him employment. You must employ him first to produce useful things; secondly, of the several (suppose equally useful) things he can equally well produce, you must set him to make that which will cause him to lead the healthiest life; lastly, of the things produced, it remains a question of wisdom and conscience how much you are to take yourself, and how much to leave to others. A large quantity, remember, unless you destroy it, *must* always

be so left at one time or another; the only questions you have to decide are, not *what* you will give, but *when*, and *how*, and to *whom*, you will give. The natural law of human life is, of course, that in youth a man shall labour and lay by store for his old age, and when age comes, shall use what he has laid by, gradually slackening his toil, and allowing himself more frank use of his store; taking care always to leave himself as much as will surely suffice for him beyond any possible length of life. What he has gained, or by tranquil and unanxious toil continues to gain, more than is enough for his own need, he ought so to administer, while he yet lives, as to see the good of it again beginning, in other hands; for thus he has himself the greatest sum of pleasure from it, and faithfully uses his sagacity in its control. Whereas most men, it appears, dislike the sight of their fortunes going out into service again, and say to themselves,—" I can indeed nowise prevent this money from falling at last into the hands of others, nor hinder the good of it from becoming theirs, not mine; but at least let a merciful death save me from being a witness of their satisfaction; and may God so far be gracious to me as to let no good come of any of this money of mine before my eyes."

153. Supposing this feeling unconquerable, the safest way of rationally indulging it would be for the capitalist at once to spend all his fortune on himself, which might actually, in many cases, be quite the rightest as well as the pleasantest thing to do, if he had just tastes and worthy passions. But, whether for himself only, or through the hands, and for the sake of others also, the law of wise life is, that the maker of the money should also be the spender of it, and spend it, approximately, all, before he dies; so that his true ambition as an economist should be, to die, not as rich, but as poor, as possible,* calculating the ebb tide of possession in true and calm proportion to the ebb tide of life. Which law, checking the wing

[* See the *Life of Fenelon.* "The labouring peasantry were at all times the objects of his tenderest care ; his palace at Cambray, with all his books and writings, being consumed by fire, he bore the misfortune with unruffled calmness, and said it was better his palace should be burnt than the cottage of a poor peasant." (These thoroughly good men always go too far, and lose their power over the mass.) He died exemplifying the mean he had always observed between prodigality and avarice, leaving neither debts nor money.]

of accumulative desire in the mid-volley,* and leading to peace of possession and fulness of fruition in old age, is also wholesome in that by the freedom of gift, together with present help and counsel, it at once endears and dignifies age in the sight of youth, which then no longer strips the bodies of the dead, but receives the grace of the living. Its chief use would (or will be, for men are indeed capable of attaining to this much use of their reason), that some temperance and measure will be put to the acquisitiveness of commerce.† For as things stand, a man holds it his duty to be temperate in his food, and of his body, but

* καὶ πενίαν ἡγουμένους εἶναι μὴ τὸ τὴν οὐσίαν ἐλάττω ποιεῖν ἀλλὰ τὸ τὴν ἀπληστίαν πλείω. "And thinking (wisely) that poverty consists not in making one's possessions less, but one's avarice more."—*Laws*, v. 8. Read the context, and compare. "He who spends for all that is noble, and gains by nothing but what is just, will hardly be notably wealthy, or distressfully poor."—*Laws*, v. 42.

† The fury of modern trade arises chiefly out of the possibility of making sudden fortunes by largeness of transaction, and accident of discovery or contrivance. I have no doubt that the final interest of every nation is to check the action of these commercial lotteries; and that all great accidental gains or losses should be national,—not individual. But speculation absolute, unconnected with commercial effort, is an unmitigated evil in a state, and the root of countless evils beside.

for no duty to be temperate in his riches, and of his mind. He sees that he ought not to waste his youth and his flesh for luxury; but he will waste his age, and his soul, for money, and think he does no wrong, nor know the *delirium tremens* of the intellect for disease. But the law of life is, that a man should fix the sum he desires to make annually, as the food he desires to eat daily; and stay when he has reached the limit, refusing increase of business, and leaving it to others, so obtaining due freedom of time for better thoughts.* How the gluttony of business is punished, a bill of health for the principals of the richest city houses, issued annually, would show in a sufficiently impressive manner.

154. I know, of course, that these statements will be received by the modern merchant as an active border rider of the sixteenth century would have heard of its being proper for men of the Marches to get their living by the spade, instead of the spur. But my business is only to state veracities and necessities; I neither look for the acceptance of the one, nor hope

[* I desire in the strongest terms to reinforce all that is contained in this paragraph]

for the nearness of the other. Near or distant, the day *will* assuredly come when the merchants of a state shall be its true ministers of exchange, its porters, in the double sense of carriers and gate-keepers, bringing all lands into frank and faithful communication, and knowing for their master of guild, Hermes the herald, instead of Mercury the gain-guarder.

155. And now, finally, for immediate rule to all who will accept it.

The distress of any population means that they need food, house-room, clothes, and fuel. You can never, therefore, be wrong in employing any labourer to produce food, house-room, clothes, or fuel; but you are *always* wrong if you employ him to produce nothing, (for then some other labourer must be worked double time to feed him); and you are generally wrong, at present, if you employ him (unless he can do nothing else) to produce works of art or luxuries; because modern art is mostly on a false basis, and modern luxury is criminally great.*

* It is especially necessary that the reader should keep his mind fixed on the methods of consumption and destruction, as the true sources of national poverty. Men are

156. The way to produce more food is mainly to bring in fresh ground, and increase facilities of carriage;—to break rock, exchange earth, drain the moist, and water the dry, to mend roads, and build harbours of refuge. Taxation thus spent will annihilate taxation, but spent in war, it annihilates revenue.

apt to call every exchange "expenditure," but it is only consumption which is expenditure. A large number of the purchases made by the richer classes are mere forms of interchange of unused property, wholly without effect on national prosperity. It matters nothing to the state whether, if a china pipkin be rated as worth a hundred pounds, A has the pipkin and B the pounds, or A the pounds and B the pipkin. But if the pipkin is pretty, and A or B breaks it, there is national loss, not otherwise. So again, when the loss has really taken place, no shifting of the shoulders that bear it will do away with the reality of it. There is an intensely ludicrous notion in the public mind respecting the abolishment of debt by denying it. When a debt is denied, the lender loses instead of the borrower, that is all; the loss is precisely, accurately, everlastingly the same. The Americans borrow money to spend in blowing up their own houses. They deny their debt, by one third already [1863], gold being at fifty premium; and they will probably deny it wholly. That merely means that the holders of the notes are to be the losers instead of the issuers. The quantity of loss is precisely equal, and irrevocable; it is the quantity of human industry spent in effecting the explosion, plus the quantity of goods exploded. Honour only decides *who* shall pay the sum lost, not whether it is to be paid or not. Paid it must be, and to the uttermost farthing.

157. The way to produce house-room is to apply your force first to the humblest dwellings. When your bricklayers are out of employ, do not build splendid new streets, but better the old ones; send your paviours and slaters to the poorest villages, and see that your poor are healthily lodged, before you try your hand on stately architecture. You will find its stateliness rise better under the trowel afterwards; and we do not yet build so well that we need hasten to display our skill to future ages. Had the labour which has decorated the Houses of Parliament filled, instead, rents in walls and roofs throughout the county of Middlesex; and our deputies met to talk within massive walls that would have needed no stucco for five hundred years,—the decoration might have been better afterwards, and the talk now. And touching even our highly conscientious church building, it may be well to remember that in the best days of church plans, their masons called themselves "logeurs du bon Dieu;" and that since, according to the most trusted reports, God spends a good deal of His time in cottages as well as in churches, He might

perhaps like to be a little better lodged there also.

158. The way to get more clothes is—not, necessarily, to get more cotton. There were words written twenty years ago * which would have saved many of us some shivering, had they been minded in time. Shall we read them again?

"The Continental people, it would seem, are importing our machinery, beginning to spin cotton, and manufacture for themselves; to cut us out of this market, and then out of that! Sad news, indeed; but irremediable. By no means the saddest news—the saddest news, is that we should find our national existence, as I sometimes hear it said, depend on selling manufactured cotton at a farthing an ell cheaper than any other people. A most narrow stand for a great nation to base itself on! A stand which, with all the Corn-Law abrogations conceivable, I do not think will be capable of enduring.

[* (*Past and Present*, Chap. IX. of Third Section.) To think that for these twenty—now twenty-six—years, this one voice of Carlyle's has been the only faithful and useful utterance in all England, and has sounded through all these years in vain! See *Fors Clavigera*, Letter X.]

"My friends, suppose we quitted that stand; suppose we came honestly down from it and said—'This is our minimum of cotton prices; we care not, for the present, to make cotton any cheaper. Do you, if it seem so blessed to you, make cotton cheaper. Fill your lungs with cotton fur, your heart with copperas fumes, with rage and mutiny; become ye the general gnomes of Europe, slaves of the lamp!' I admire a nation which fancies it will die if it do not undersell all other nations to the end of the world. Brothers, we will cease to undersell them; we will be content to equal-sell them; to be happy selling equally with them! I do not see the use of underselling them: cotton-cloth is already twopence a yard, or lower; and yet bare backs were never more numerous among us. Let inventive men cease to spend their existence incessantly contriving how cotton can be made cheaper; and try to invent a little how cotton at its present cheapness could be somewhat justlier divided among us.

"Let inventive men consider—whether the secret of this universe does after all consist in making money. With a hell which means—

'failing to make money,' I do not think there is any heaven possible that would suit one well. In brief, all this Mammon gospel of supply-and-demand, competition, *laissez faire*, and devil take the hindmost" (foremost, is it not, rather, Mr. Carlyle?), "begins to be one of the shabbiest gospels ever preached."

159. The way to produce more fuel* is first to make your coal mines safer, by sinking more shafts; then set all your convicts to work in them, and if, as is to be hoped, you succeed in diminishing the supply of that sort of labourer, consider what means there may be, first, of growing forest where its growth will improve climate; secondly, of splintering the forests which now make continents of fruitful land pathless and poisonous, into faggots for fire;—so gaining at once dominion icewards and sunwards. Your steam power has been given (you will find eventually) for work such as that: and not for excursion trains, to give the labourer a moment's breath, at the peril of his breath for ever, from amidst the

[* We don't want to produce more fuel just now, but much less; and to use what we get for cooking and warming ourselves, instead of for running from place to place.]

cities which it has crushed into masses of corruption. When you know how to build cities, and how to rule them, you will be able to breathe in their streets, and the "excursion" will be the afternoon's walk or game in the fields round them.

160. "But nothing of this work will pay?"

No; no more than it pays to dust your rooms, or wash your doorsteps. It will pay; not at first in currency, but in that which is the end and the source of currency,—in life; (and in currency richly afterwards). It will pay in that which is more than life,—in light, whose true price has not yet been reckoned in any currency, and yet into the image of which, all wealth, one way or other, must be cast. For your riches must either be as the lightning, which,

> Begot but in a cloud,
> Though shining bright, and speaking loud,
> Whilst it begins, concludes its violent race;
> And, where it gilds, it wounds the place;—

or else, as the lightning of the sacred sign, which shines from one part of the heaven to the other. There is no other choice; you must either take dust for deity, spectre for

possession, fettered dream for life, and for epitaph, this reversed verse of the great Hebrew hymn of economy (Psalm cxii.):—
"He hath gathered together, he hath stripped the poor, his iniquity remaineth for ever:"—or else, having the sun of justice to shine on you, and the sincere substance of good in your possession, and the pure law and liberty of life within you, leave men to write this better legend over your grave:—

"He hath dispersed abroad. He hath given to the poor. His righteousness remaineth for ever."

APPENDICES.

[I HAVE brought together in these last pages a few notes, which were not properly to be incorporated with the text, and which, at the bottom of pages, checked the reader's attention to the main argument. They contain, however, several statements to which I wish to be able to refer, or have already referred, in other of my books, so that I think right to preserve them.]

APPENDIX I.—(p. 7.)

THE greatest of all economists are those most opposed to the doctrine of "laissez faire," namely, the fortifying virtues, which the wisest men of all time have arranged under the general heads of Prudence, or Discretion (the spirit which discerns and adopts rightly); Justice (the spirit which rules and divides rightly); Fortitude (the spirit which persists and endures rightly); and Temperance (the spirit which stops and refuses rightly). These cardinal and sentinel virtues are not only the means of protecting and prolonging life itself, but they are the chief guards, or sources, of the material means of life, and the governing powers and princes of economy. Thus, precisely according to the number of just men in a nation, is their power of avoiding either intestine or foreign war. All disputes may be peaceably settled, if a sufficient number of persons have been trained to submit to the principles of justice, while the necessity for war is in direct ratio to the number of unjust persons who are incapable of determining a quarrel but by violence. Whether the injustice take the form of the desire of dominion, or of refusal to submit to it, or of lust of territory, or lust of money, or of mere irregular passion and wanton will, the result is economically the same;—loss of the quantity of power and life consumed in repressing the injustice added to the material and moral destruction caused by the fact of war. The early civil wars of England, and the existing * war in America, are curious examples—these under monarchical, this under republican, institutions—of the results

[* Written in 1862. I little thought that when I next corrected my type, the "existing" war best illustrative of the sentence, would be between Frenchmen in the Elysian Fields of Paris.]

on large masses of nations of the want of education in principles of justice. But the mere dread of distrust resulting from the want of the inner virtues of Faith and Charity prove often no less costly than war itself. The fear which France and England have of each other costs each nation about fifteen millions sterling annually, besides various paralyses of commerce; that sum being spent in the manufacture of means of destruction instead of means of production. There is no more reason in the nature of things that France and England should be hostile to each other than that England and Scotland should be, or Lancashire and Yorkshire; and the reciprocal terrors of the opposite sides of the English Channel are neither more necessary, more economical, nor more virtuous, than the old riding and reiving on the opposite flanks of the Cheviots, or than England's own weaving for herself of crowns of thorn, from the stems of her Red and White Roses.

APPENDIX II.—(p. 30.)

FEW passages of the book which at least some part of the nations at present most advanced in civilisation accept as an expression of final truth, have been more distorted than those bearing on Idolatry. For the idolatry there denounced is neither sculpture, nor veneration of sculpture. It is simply the substitution of an "Eidolon," phantasm, or imagination of Good, for that which is real and enduring; from the Highest Living Good, which gives life, to the lowest material good which ministers to it. The Creator, and the things created, which He is said to have "seen good" in creating, are in this their eternal goodness appointed always to be "worshipped,"—*i.e.*, to have goodness and worth ascribed to them from the heart; and the sweep and range of idolatry extend to the rejection of any or all of these, "calling evil good, and good evil,—putting bitter for sweet, and sweet for bitter."* For in that rejection and substitution we betray the first of all Loyalties, to the fixed Law of life, and with resolute opposite loyalty serve our own imagination of good, which is the law, not of the House, but of the Grave (otherwise called the law of "mark missing," which we translate "law of Sin"); these "two masters," between whose services we have to choose, being otherwise distinguished as God and Mammon, which Mammon, though we narrowly take it as the power of money only, is in truth the great evil Spirit of false and fond desire, or "Covetousness, which is Idolatry." So that Iconoclasm—*image*-breaking —is easy; but an Idol cannot be broken—it must

---

* Compare the close of the Fourth Lecture in *Aratra Pentelici*.

be forsaken; and this is not so easy, either to do, or persuade to doing. For men may readily be convinced of the weakness of an image; but not of the emptiness of an imagination.

APPENDIX III.—(p. 34.)

I HAVE not attempted to support, by the authority of other writers, any of the statements made in these papers; indeed, if such authorities were rightly collected, there would be no occasion for my writing at all. Even in the scattered passages referring to this subject in three books of Carlyle's —Sartor Resartus, Past and Present, and the Latter Day Pamphlets,—all has been said that needs to be said, and far better than I shall ever say it again. But the habit of the public mind at present is to require everything to be uttered diffusely, loudly, and a hundred times over, before it will listen; and it has revolted against these papers of mine as if they contained things daring and new, when there is not one assertion in them of which the truth has not been for ages known to the wisest, and proclaimed by the most eloquent of men. It would be [I had written *will* be; but have now reached a time of life for which there is but one mood—the conditional,] a far greater pleasure to me hereafter, to collect their words than to add to mine; Horace's clear rendering of the substance of the passages in the text may be found room for at once,

> Si quis emat citharas, emptas comportet in unum
> Nec studio citharae, nec Musae deditus ulli ;
> Si scalpra et formas non sutor, nautica vela
> Aversus mercaturis, delirus et amens
> Undique dicatur merito. Qui discrepat istis
> Qui nummos aurumque recondit, nescius uti
> Compositis ; metuensque velut contingere sacrum ?

[Which may be roughly thus translated :—

"Were anybody to buy fiddles, and collect a number, being in no wise given to fiddling, nor fond of music: or if, being no cobbler, he collected awls and lasts, or, having no mind for sea-adventure, bought sails, every one would call him a madman, and deservedly. But what difference is there between such a man and one who lays by coins and gold, and does not know how to use, when he has got them?"]

With which it is perhaps desirable also to give Xenophon's statement, it being clearer than any English one can be, owing to the power of the general Greek term for wealth, "useable things."

[I have cut out the Greek because I can't be troubled to correct the accents, and am always nervous about them; here it is in English, as well as I can do it :—

"This being so, it follows that things are only

property to the man who knows how to use them; as flutes, for instance, are property to the man who can pipe upon them respectably; but to one who knows not how to pipe, they are no property, unless he can get rid of them advantageously. . . . For if they are not sold, the flutes are no property (being serviceable for nothing); but, sold, they become property. To which Socrates made answer, —'and only then if he knows how to sell them, for if he sell them to another man who cannot play on them, still they are no property.'"]

APPENDIX IV.—(p. 38.)

THE reader is to include here in the idea of "Government," any branch of the Executive, or even any body of private persons, entrusted with the practical management of public interests unconnected directly with their own personal ones. In theoretical discussions of legislative interference with political economy, it is usually, and of course unnecessarily, assumed that Government must be always of that form and force in which we have been accustomed to see it;—that its abuses can never be less, nor its wisdom greater, nor its powers more numerous. But, practically, the custom in most civilized countries is, for every man to deprecate the interference of Government as long as things tell for his personal advantage, and to call for it when they cease to do so. The request of the Manchester Economists to be supplied with cotton by Government (the system of supply and demand having, for the time, fallen sorrowfully short of the expectations of scientific persons from it), is an interesting case in point. It were to be wished that less wide and bitter suffering, suffering, too, of the innocent, had been needed to force the nation, or some part of it, to ask itself why a body of men, already confessedly capable of managing matters both military and divine, should not be permitted, or even requested, at need, to provide in some wise for sustenance as well as for defence; and secure, if it might be,—(and it might, I think, even the *rather* be),—purity of bodily, as well as of spiritual, aliment? Why, having made many roads for the passage of armies, may they not make a few for the conveyance of food; and after organising, with applause, various schemes of theological instruction for the Public, organise, moreover, some methods of bodily nourishment for them? Or is the soul so much less trustworthy in its instincts than the stomach, that legislation is necessary for the one, but inapplicable to the other?

APPENDIX V.—(p. 104.)

I DEBATED with myself whether to make the note on Homer longer by examining the typical meaning of the shipwreck of Ulysses, and his escape from Charybdis by help of her figtree; but as I should have had to go on to the lovely myth of Leucothea's veil, and did not care to spoil this by a hurried account of it, I left it for future examination; and, three days after the paper was published, observed that the reviewers, with their customary helpfulness, were endeavouring to throw the whole subject back into confusion by dwelling on the single (as they imagined) oversight. I omitted also a note on the sense of the word λυγρὸν, with respect to the pharmacy of Circe, and herb-fields of Helen (compare its use in Odyssey, xvii., 473, etc.), which would farther have illustrated the nature of the Circean power. But, not to be led too far into the subtleties of these myths, observe respecting them all, that even in very simple parables, it is not always easy to attach indisputable meaning to every part of them. I recollect some years ago, throwing an assembly of learned persons who had met to delight themselves with interpretations of the parable of the prodigal son, (interpretations which had up to that moment gone very smoothly), into mute indignation, by inadvertently asking who the *un*prodigal son was, and what was to be learned by *his* example. The leading divine of the company, Mr. Molyneux, at last explained to me that the unprodigal son was a lay figure, put in for dramatic effect, to make the story prettier, and that no note was to be taken of him. Without, however, admitting that Homer put in the last escape of Ulysses merely to make his story prettier, this is nevertheless true of all Greek myths, that they have many opposite lights and shades; they are as changeful as opal, and like opal, usually have one colour by reflected, and another by transmitted light. But they are true jewels for all that, and full of noble enchantment for those who can use them; for those who cannot, I am content to repeat the words I wrote four years ago, in the appendix to the *Two Paths*—

"The entire purpose of a great thinker may be difficult to fathom, and we may be over and over again more or less mistaken in guessing at his meaning; but the real, profound, nay, quite bottomless and unredeemable mistake, is the fool's thought, that he had *no* meaning."

APPENDIX VI.—(p. 121.)

THE derivation of words is like that of rivers; there is one real source, usually small, unlikely, and difficult to find, far up among the hills; then, as the word flows on and comes into service, it takes in the force of other words from other sources, and becomes quite another word—often much more than one word, after the junction—a word as it were of many waters, sometimes both sweet and bitter. Thus the whole force of our English "charity" depends on the guttural in "charis" getting confused with the c of the Latin "carus;" thenceforward throughout the middle ages, the two ideas ran on together, and both got confused with St. Paul's ἀγάπη, which expresses a different idea in all sorts of ways; our "charity" having not only brought in the entirely foreign sense of almsgiving, but lost the essential sense of contentment, and lost much more in getting too far away from the "charis" of the final gospel benedictions. For truly it is fine Christianity we have come to, which, professing to expect the perpetual grace or charity of its Founder, has not itself grace or charity enough to hinder it from overreaching its friends in sixpenny bargains; and which, supplicating evening and morning the forgiveness of its own debts, goes forth at noon to take its fellow-servants by the throat, saying,—not merely "Pay me that thou owest," but "Pay me that thou owest me *not*."

It is true that we sometimes wear Ophelia's rue with a difference, and call it "Herb o' grace o' Sundays," taking consolation out of the offertory with—"Look, what he layeth out, it shall be paid him again." Comfortable words indeed, and good to set against the old royalty of Largesse—

> Whose moste joie was, I wis,
> When that she gave, and said, "Have this."

[I am glad to end, for this time, with these lovely words of Chaucer. We have heard only too much lately of "Indiscriminate charity," with implied reproval, not of the Indiscrimination merely, but of the Charity also. We have partly succeeded in enforcing on the minds of the poor the idea that it is disgraceful to receive; and are likely, without much difficulty, to succeed in persuading not a few of the rich that it is disgraceful to give. But the political economy of a great state makes both giving and receiving graceful; and the political economy of true religion interprets the saying that "it is more blessed to give than to receive," not as the promise of reward in another life for mortified selfishness in this, but as pledge of bestowal upon us of that sweet and better nature, which does not mortify itself in giving.]

BRANTWOOD, CONISTON,
5th October, 1871.

INDEX

INDEX

(The references are not to pages but to the sections which are common to all editions of the book. The sections in the preface are, however, added for the first time in this edition. Where the words "*orig. ess.*" are added in brackets after a reference, they indicate that the passage referred to is peculiar to the original form of the work, as it appeared in *Fraser's Magazine* under the title of "Essays in Political Economy.")

Actions, right, seen in beauty of countenance, 6.
Aglaia, Charis, wife of Vulcan, 101.
Agriculture, as dominion over land and sea (fixed and flowing fields), 16 (*orig. ess.*).
,, volunteer, proposed, 149.
Ambition and love of money, Dante on, 93.
Ambrosia, not to be had without labour, 94.
America, Carlyle on, 124.
,, condition of, "the greatest railroad accident on record," 124.
,, dollar-worship in, App. I. (*orig. ess.*).
,, explosions in, 47, 56.
,, has no republic or institutions, 124.
,, loan in (1863), 155 *n.*
,, slavery in, 131.
,, war in, 124 *n.* A. I. (*orig. ess.*).
Ames, on monarchy and republics, quoted by Emerson, 124 *n.*
Apathy, modern, its baseness, 108.
Aphrodite, birth of, 101.
Apollo's rule, οὐ πληγῇ νέμων, 130.
Architecture, all houses to be well, before any finely, built, 157.
Archons and archic law, 110-17.
Aristocracy, government by, 123.
Aristophanes, κάπηλοι ἀσπίδων, 127.
Art, great, only possible in climates where life is in open air, 96.
,, may be a means to great wealth, 139 *n.*
,, modern, false basis of, 155.
,, works of, accumulated by a prosperous nation, 54.
,, ,, economical value of, 20.
,, ,, included in list of things valuable, 15.
,, ,, prices given for, 65.

Art, works of, possession of, laws as to, 115.
Arve (Savoy), inundation of the, 147.
  ,,   ,, miserable dwellings in the plain of, 150 seq.
Athena's rule, οὐ πληγῇ νέμων, 130.
Athens, purity of coinage, 77 *n*.
Avarice, Dante on, 88.
Austrians in Venice and the works of Tintoret (1851), *pref.* 3, 9.
Author (1.) *Personal;* (2.) *Teaching;* (3.) *Books of, quoted or referred to:*—
  (1.) accuses himself of vanity, 100 *n*.
      as a boy, at his father's table, hearing of national debt, *pref.* 18.
      cottage on plain of Arve, repaired by, 151.
      Greek accents and, App. III.
      servants of, would serve him for nothing, *pref.* 12.
      taking daguerreotypes at Venice, 77 *n*.
      in Venice, 1851, *pref.* 3.
      checked in his work, 1863, *pref.* 20.
      writes "Munera Pulveris" in Switzerland, 1862-3, winter, *pref.* 22.
      Bran wood, Oct. 5, 1871, App. VI.
      on relief of Paris committee (1871), *pref.* 10.
      Denmark Hill, Nov. 25, 1871, *pref.* 23.
  (2.) Teaching, on prodigal and unprodigal son, App. VI.
      plans of, unfulfilled, 57 *n*.
      political economy of, defined, *pref.* 13.
      ,,   ,, does not put sentiment for science, *pref.* 13; 99 and *n*.
      ,,   ,, plan to write an exhaustive treatise on, *pref.* 20.
      ,,   ,, recognition of true wealth (Tintorets). *pref.* 3-4.
      ,,   ,, Utopian! 148.
      ,,   ,, weary of reiterating its truths, 96 *n*.
      style of, affected concentration ("Munera Pulveris"), *pref.* 22.
      ,, uses metaphor for brevity, 83 *n*.
      ,, translates literally, 105 *n*.
      ,, use of words, 125 *n*.
      teaching of, true, and his hope of its fulfilment, 154.
  (3.) Books of, quoted or referred to—
      Aratra Pentelici, Lect. IV., Idolatry, App. II.
      Fors Clavigera, aim of, *pref.* 21.
      ,,   ,, notes on etymology in, 100 *n*.
      ,,   ,, Letter X., 158 *n*.
      Lectures on Art, on Tintoret, *pref.* 4.

INDEX.

Modern Painters, Vol. V. p. 255, faith and πειθω, App. VI.
Munera Pulveris, method of its argument, 43.
,, ,, original scope of, *pref.* 20.
,, ,, criticism of, absurd, 69 *n.* App. III. V.
,, ,, dedicated to Carlyle, *pref.* 22.
,, ,, *Fraser's Magazine* and, *pref.* 20 ; 94.
,, ,, style of, its faults, *pref.* 22.
,, ,, teaching of, the first English treatise on true political economy, *pref.* 1.
,, ,, how written and when, *pref.* 22, 30.
,, ,, carefully revised and why, *pref.* 22.
,, ,, misprints in original essays, App. V. VI. (*orig. ess.*).
,, ,, passage on Dante, praised by editor of *Fraser's Magazine*, 94.
,, ,, one sentence in, questioned by author, 112 and *n.*
,, ,, paras. 137-9 insisted on, 138 *n.*
Political Economy of Art (A Joy for Ever), on luxury in dress, quoted, *pref.* 16.
Sesame and Lilies, dedicated to φιλή, *pref.* 22.
Two Paths, on meaning of great writers, App. V.
Unto this Last, reception of, *pref.* 20.
,, ,, quoted, p. 115, 63 *n.*
,, ,, ,, on education, 108 (*orig. ess.*). 59 *n.* (*orig. ess.*).
,, ,, ,, p. 81, on price, 62 *n.* (*orig. ess.*).

BACCHUS, the grave, 102 *n.*
Bacon, "Advancement of Learning," 124 *n.* (*orig. ess.*).
,, on Charybdis, 86.
,, political economy of, 2.
,, on the Sirens, 90.
,, on usury, "concessum propter duritiem cordis," 98.
Βαναυσία, Plato and Xenophon on, 109 *n.*
Baptism, moral, with water and fire, 106.
Beauty, personal, the result of right action, and *vice versâ*, 6.
Bedford missal, the, 65.
Beetles, flight of, on Lake of Zug, and democracy, 126.
Benediction, "grace, mercy, and peace," 106.
Bible :—
  Gen. i. 10. Saw that it was good. App. II.
  Gen. xxvii. 41. The days of mourning for my father . . . brother, 69.
  Ps. cxii. 9. He hath dispersed abroad, 160.
  ,, cxix. 25. My soul cleaveth unto the dust, 88.
  Prov. xix. 17. Look what he layeth out . . . paid again, App. VI.
  Isaiah ii. 4. Spears into pruning hooks, 52.
  ,, v. 20. Calling evil good, and good evil,—putting bitter for sweet, App. II.

Bible, *continued* :—
    Isaiah xxxvi. 8.   I will give thee a thousand horses . . . riders on them, 35.
    Lam. iii. 27.   It is good for a man that he bear the yoke in his youth, 112.
    Matt. v. 3.   Blessed are the poor in spirit, 56 *n*.
    ,, vi. 25.   Is not life more than meat, 56.
    ,, xiii. 22.   ἀπατὴ πλούτου, 90.
    ,, xviii. 28.   Pay me that thou owest, App. VI.
    ,, xix. 8.   Because of the hardness of your hearts, 98.
    ,, xxi. 19.   Barren fig-tree, 93.
    Luke vi. 24.   You that are rich . . . received consolation, 56 *n*.
    ,, xii. 18.   I will pull down my barns . . . greater, 72.
    ,, xv. 11, seq.   Prodigal son, App. V.
    Acts xx. 35.   More blessed to give, App. VI.
    Rom. viii. 21.   Bondage of corruption, 103.

Bibliomania, 65.
Biography, 122.
Birds, Chaucer and Cowley on, 149 *n*.
  ,, shooting of, 149.
Blink Bonny (horse), 65.
Body and soul not really opposed, 6.
Books, their economical value, 19. See s. *Bibliomania*.
Buildings, their value in (1) permanent strength, (2) association and beauty, 17.
Building land, modern view of suitable, 79.
British Association, on absorption of gold, 77 *n*.
British Museum, a treasury, not a school, 115, 122.
  ,,   ,, what it is and is not, 115, 122.

CAFFIRS, England and the, 97 *n*.
Canacé's falcon, 149 *n*.
Cancan, the modern dance, *pref.* 4.
Capital limits labour, untrue, 50.
Capitalists and foreign loans, *pref.* 19.
  ,, as mere money-chests, 38.
  ,, to do unselfish work, 147.
Caprice has no law, 34.
Caractacus, 65.
Carlyle, author's main helper in work, *pref.* 22.
  ,, dedication of "Munera Pulveris" to, *pref.* 22.
  ,, eulogy of his teaching, and its rejection, *pref.* 23.
  ,, political economy of, *pref.* 20.
  ,, quoted, on America, 124.
  ,, "Latter-day Pamphlets," 135, App. III.
  ,, "Past and Present," on permanence, 135, App. III.
  ,, ,, ,, on clothing and cotton, 158, App. I, II.
  ,, "Sartor Resartus," App. III.
Carpentry. See s. *Joiner*.
Cephalopod, the (animal), 38 (*orig. ess.*).
Charis, etymology of, 101 *n*.

INDEX. 225

Charity, etymology of, and words connected with, App. VI.
  ,,   indiscriminate, App. VI.
Charybdis, true meaning of the myth (Bacon on), 86, 93.
Chaucer, enigmatic, 87.
  ,,   on birds, 149 *n*.
  ,,   on largesse, App. VI.
  ,,   villany of, 121 *n*.
Cheapness, no such thing as, without error or wrong, 62 *n*.
  ,,   no excuse for bad things, 17 *n*.
  ,,   of glutted market, a disease, 62 *n*.
Cheating our neighbours is possible, but is not life or nature, 10.
Cherish, etymology of the word, 102.
Choir, etymology of the word, 102.
Christ washing disciples' feet, its meaning, 108.
Christianity, modern, and greed of money ("Pay me that thou owest—not"), App. VI.
Church building, modern craze for, 157.
  ,,   ,,   old masons "logeurs du bon Dieu," 157.
Cid, the, his horse, 35.
Cicero's political economy, 2.
  ,,   quoted, 60 *n*.
  ,,   ,,   Catiline, "non aquâ sed ruinâ," 124.
Circe, fable of, its meaning, 103.
  ,,   not a Siren, her power and function, 91 seq. App. V.
Cities to have fields round them, 159.
Claudian's pearl, 159 (*orig. ess.*).
Clothing the poor, 155 seq.
Coinage, purity of, in noble states, 78 *n*. See s. *Athens, Currency*.
Commerce as the agency of exchange, 95, 98.
  ,,   fury of modern, 153 *n*.
  ,,   most important to northern countries, 95.
  ,,   no profit in true, 99.
  ,,   not degrading, 101.
  ,,   the inhumanity of mercenary, 100.
  ,,   the law of international, 97.
Competition to measure wages, a bestial theory, 136 *n*.
Consols. See s. *Funds*.
Cornhill Magazine and "Unto this Last," *pref.* 20.
Corruptio optimi, *e.g.*, in commerce, 100.
Cost defined as the amount of labour necessary to obtain a thing, 60.
  ,,   intrinsic and effectual, 61.
  ,,   is price, when demand is constant, 63.
  ,,   the noblest things cost the least, 60.
Cotton, cheap, and rags common, Carlyle on, 158.
  ,,   government asked to supply Manchester with, App. IV.
Countenance, beauty of, and rightness of action, 6.
Cowley on birds, 149 *n*.
Crœsus, 27.

Credit means creed, 81 (*orig. ess. n.*).
,, -power of currency, 80.
Creed, use and meaning of the word, 81 (*orig. ess. n.*).
Crime, cost of, and of judgment, 116.
,, modern, a national disgrace, 108.
Criminals to do lowest forms of mechanical work, 109.
,, to work in mines, 159.
Critic law, its functions, 116.
Currency, bases of, better than gold, 77 seq.
,, ,, to be small, indestructible, valuable, 74 seq.
,, ,, to be pure, 77.
,, credit-power of, on what dependent, 69.
,, defined, chief definition, 69 *n*. seq.
,, ,, "expression of price in any given article," 64.
,, ,, "the claim to equivalent of anything, anywhere, at any time," 70 seq.
,, ,, transferable acknowledgment of debt, 81.
,, forced, is taxation in disguise, 78.
,, gold withdrawn from, its effect, 81 *n*.
,, holders of the, 66.
,, increase of the, its effect on industry and wealth, 24.
,, ,, often a form of taxation, 24.
,, ,, laws of, 21 seq.
,, medium of exchange, 66.
,, national habits as affecting, 67.
,, national store and, 81 seq.
,, national, and value of, 64 seq.
,, power of, fourfold (credit, real worth, exchange, labour), 80 seq.
,, ,, increased by constant exchange, 85.
,, purity of, 77 *n*.
,, soundness of = enlarging debt and means, 82.
,, transferableness of, 69.
,, true and false, distinct from strong and weak, 65.
,, value of, how affected, 58.
,, ,, and its rise and fall, 41 seq.
,, and effectual value, 39.
,, vitality and feebleness of, how tested, 70.
,, wealth, and accumulation of, made possible by, 72.
Custom, establishment of a, 106.
,, noble and base, action and indolence, 107.
,, "hangs upon us like a weight," 107.

DANTE, enigmas of, 87.
,, on avarice and prodigality, 88.
,, ,, fortune's ball in, 100 *n*.
,, ,, the power of money, 58.
,, ,, use and abuse of riches, 88 seq.
,, ,, usury, 88.

Dante, scorn of the populace, on what based, 109 *n*.
,,   similes of, their truth, 58.
      Quoted:—
         Inf. vii., 88.
         Inf. xi. Cahors (usury), 98 *n*.
            ,,   Plutus "gran nemico," 90, A. I. (*orig. ess.*).
            ,,   Sirens, 90.
            ,,   Siren of Riches, 90.
            ,,   the death of Ulysses, 93.
         Inf. xvii., 88.
         Paradise, 88.
         Purg. xix., 88.
Dear, etymology of, 101 *n*.
Death, desire to die rich, 153.
Debt and credit, duty and creed, 81 (*orig ess. n.*).
Deficiencies and efficiencies, 119.
Delphic oracle, $\pi\hat{\eta}\mu'$ $\dot{\epsilon}\pi\grave{\iota}$ $\pi\dot{\eta}\mu\alpha\tau\iota$, 127 *n*.
Demand, economy not based on supply and, 53.
   ,,   in political economy, defined as affecting price, 63.
   ,,   supply and, Carlyle on, 158.
   ,,   ,,   Manchester cotton and, App. IV.
   ,,   what we ought to, an ethical question, 84.
Democracy and republic, distinct, 124.
   ,,   illustrated by flight of beetles, 126.
Desire, the objects of right, alone are wealth, 34.
Didicisse *fideliter* artes, 124 *n*. (*orig. ess.*).
Dieu et *mon* droit, 113 *n*. (*orig. ess.*).
Dishonesty and speculation in finance, 79.
Divine Right, the true, 105.
Doge, meaning of, 125 *n*.
Draco, his name apt, 120.
Dreams of great poets and writers, 134.
Dress, luxury of, does it enrich a nation? *pref.* 15 seq.
   ,,   ,,   instance of parents ruined by their daughter's, *pref.* 16.
Duke, its meaning (ducal monarchy), 125 *n*.
Duty, use and meaning of the word, 81 (*orig. ess. n.*).

ECONOMY. See s. *Political Economy*.
Education, aim of true, 106.
   ,,   ,,   to teach men to do right, 130.
   ,,   defined, not science or knowledge, but training of character, 106.
   ,,   ,,   peace, pity, and grace implied by, 108.
   ,,   economy of words part of, 101 *n*.
   ,,   laws of, English feeling against, 112.
   ,,   may develop inherited qualities, 6.
Effort, labour is not mere, but suffering in effort, 59.
Emerson, quoted, on monarchy and republics, 124 *n*.

Employment, laws of, 152.
,, practical rules for, 155.
England, early civil wars of, App. I.
,, fear of France in, its annual cost, App. I.
,, feeling in, against educational law, 112.
,, slavery in modern, 131.
,, wealth and poverty of, do they balance each other? 57.
Enigmas of great poets and writers, 87.
Equality, the cry for, not irreverence, but folly, 121.
Equivalence of money and money value, 40.
Etymology, interest of, 100 *n*.
Evil never produces good, 33.
Exchange in commerce, costly, and therefore to be limited, 98.
,, power of money, 80.
Excursion trains, 159.
Expenditure and exchange, distinct, 155 *n*.
,, selfish and unselfish, 147.

FAITH, etymology and use of the word, 81 (*orig. ess.*), App. V. VI. (*orig. ess.*).
,, works, and modern dispute on, App. VI. (*orig. ess.*).
Fawcett's " Political Economy," national questions not touched in, *pref.* 15.
,, ,, ,, on national debt and consols, *pref.* 18.
,, ,, ,, on rent, *pref.* 17.
Feat and defeat in labour, 59.
Fenelon, Life of, 153 *n*.
Fig-tree, the barren, in Homer and Dante, 93.
Finance, simple enough, to cool heads and honest hearts, 79.
Fine, and "fine" English and French, 134.
Fireworks, national store of, its value, 47.
Fish, climbing perch, 126.
Food, economy of, 18.
Fors *v.* mors, 118.
,, words connected with, 100 *n*.
Fortune, acquiring of, a form of taxing the poor, 139.
,, making of sudden, 153 *n*.
,, the wheel of, 100 *n*.
France, fear of England, App. I.
,, German war with, 96 *n*. App. I. *n*.
,, luxury of, its example to England, *pref.* 16.
Franchise, proposals for, to be universal, not equal, 129.
Fraser's Magazine and "Munera Pulveris," *pref.* 20, 94.
Fraud, loss of time spent in, 104.
Freedom, restraint and true, 103.
Free-trade, protection and encouragement, App. IV. (*orig. ess.*).
Funds, national, advantages of, *pref.* 19; 38. See s. *National store*.

GENEVA watches, and wealth, 49.
Goethe speaks in enigmas, 87.
    Quoted:—
        Faust, Part II., Plutus in, 88.
        Lemures, "Wer hat das Haus so schlecht gebeaut?" 149.
Gold as a medium of currency, 74 seq.
  ,, effect of withdrawing it from the currency, 81 *n.*
  ,, labour wasted in obtaining, 75 *n.*
  ,, use of, only in arts (ornament), not for money, 77 *n.*
  ,, value of, coined and uncoined, 69.
  ,, ,, its depreciation, 76.
Good and evil are fixed and absolute, 32.
Government, always costly, 127.
  ,, by council, visible and invisible, 122.
  ,, consists in custom, laws, and councils, 106.
  ,, firmness more than form of, 125.
  ,, forms of, monarchy, democracy, oligarchy, 123.
  ,, "for forms of government . . ." its truth shown, 125.
  ,, history of a, not always that of the nation, 122.
  ,, interference of, when objected to, when called for, App. IV.
  ,, names of different, confused and misused nowadays, 123 seq.
  ,, national store of wealth to be kept by, 41.
  ,, policy of all (whatever its form), "the wise to rule the unwise," 125.
  ,, railways, &c., to be under, 128.
Graces, the, their function, &c., 101 seq.
Gratis and gratia, 100.
Great men go too far in goodness, and so lose influence, 153 *n.*
Greek myths, full of meaning, App. V.
  ,, tragedians, enigmatic utterances of, 87.

HABIT, meaning of the word, 106.
Happiness, a cause and effect of life, 5.
Heredity of moral and physical qualities, 6.
Herbert, George, quoted:—
        "Lift up thy head," &c., 89.
        "Correct thy passion," &c., 103.
Hincksey diggings, foreshadowed, 109, 149.
Histoire d'une Bouchée de Pain, quoted, 91.
History, a nation's, not always that of its government, 122.
Holy Ghost, means "helpful and honest," 101 *n.*
Homer, enigmatic, 87.
  ,, Plato's distrust of, 87.
  ,, scorn of the populace in, on what based, 109 *n.*

Homer, quoted or referred to :—
 Arete, 134.
 Circe and the swine, 91.
 Hephæstus and Venus, its meaning, 101.
 Phæacia, meaning of, 101.
 Scylla and Charybdis, meaning of, 93-4.
 Ulysses' shipwreck, App. V.
 Sirens, 90, 92.
 ὡς δ'ὅτ ὀπωριvὸς, &c., 124 *n*.

Honesty, the best policy, truth of, 104.
Horace, quoted :—
 pinguis Phæaxque, 101.
 odi profanum, 109 *n*.
 vaga arena—numero carentis, } 134 (*orig. ess.*)
 animo rotundum percupisse?
 Si quis emat citharas, &c., App. III.

Horse-mania, English, why no word for, as for biblio-mania, 65.

IDOLATRY, of things and of the phantasm of good, App. II.
Ignorance, no science of, 34.
Ill-th and health, 37.
Indignation, true punishment and just, 120-1.
Influence of men, invisible, 122.
Iniquity, its general meaning, 110 *n*.
Injury, defined, the worst, unconscious and due to indolence, 117-8.
Instinct of reverence and wrath, 121.
Instruments, their value in what, 17.
International fears—one nation of another, App. I.
 ,, values, and their one law, 96 *n*. 97.
Inundation, as illustrating political economy and wages, 141.
 ,, of the Arve (Savoy), scheme to check, 147.

JOINER, English, at work on London house, useless precision, 151.
Judge, his offices of reward and punishment, 111.
Justice, personal and purchased, 116.
 ,, principles of, and education, App. I.

KINGS as lawgivers, 111.
 ,, can do no wrong (in what sense true), 113.
 ,, "divine right" of, 113 (*orig. ess. n.*).
 ,, "rex eris si recte facies," 105.

LABOUR, capital limits, untrue, 50.
 ,, defined as the contest of man with an opposite, 59.
 ,, ,, is not effort, but suffering in effort, 59.
 ,, ,, "that quantity of our toil which we die in," 59.

INDEX. 231

Labour, division of, its principles illustrated, 63.
,, economy of, not sale, to be considered by Political Economy, 59.
,, kinds of, in different climates, 96.
,, law of, in youth and age, 152.
,, manual (especially agricultural) to be done by upper classes, 109.
,, money's power over, 80.
,, not to be bought or sold, 59.
,, the origin of value, *pref.* 5.
Laissez faire and aller, baseness of modern, 108.
,, ,, doctrine, App. I.
,, ,, Carlyle on, 158.
Land, best, that most beautiful in men, animals, and flowers, 16.
,, its enjoyment cannot, like money, be monopolized, 85.
,, ownership of, *pref.* 17.
,, the people driven off the, in England, 131 *n*.
,, value of, physically (in produce), intellectually (in beauty), 16.
,, waste, 115.
,, ,, to be brought in by volunteer labour, 149.
Language, accurate and loose use of, its effect, 101 *n*.
Largesse, Chaucer on, App. VI.
Law, archic, meristic, and critic, 110–6.
,, art of, a noble discipline and profession, 106.
,, cost of national, 116.
,, educational, not criminal only, 112.
,, fatal character of all, 110 *n*.
,, formatory, not reformatory, 112.
,, impossible for it to cover all points of conduct, 112.
,, to regulate keeping of land, water, and air, 115.
,, cannot remedy political mischief, 98.
,, to enforce security of property, 67.
,, true scientific, and false political economy, xiv. 12.
,, stands by right alone, 113.
,, is either statute or judgment, 111.
Lawyers, the profession of the law, felt to be noble, 116.
Leucothea's veil, App. V.
Liberty, true, is in restraint, 103.
Libraries, free, to be established, 115.
Life, a cause and effect of happiness, 5.
,, healthy and happy, the end of political economy, 5.
,, human, is naturally harmonious, 6.
,, the law of human, and work, 10.
,, what things shorten or prolong man's, 8.
Lincolnshire coast to be embanked, 149.
Lithographs, and Tintorets, their relative value, *pref.* 5.
Loans, foreign, and wars, 19.
,, national, their nature, 38.

Love, capacity for infinite, in man, 121.
,, comes only from harmony, 102.
Lower classes, are they really lower? 109 *n*.
Lucian, on sale of lives, 132 *n*.
Lucum ligna, 124.
Luxury, does it benefit the poor, *pref.* 16.
,, economy of, 18.
,, modern, criminally great, 155.
,, producing of, is not wealth, *ib.*

MACHINERY, its true value and proper work, 17.
Maintenance of a state, defined, 3.
Mammon, true meaning of, App. II.
Man, difference between man and, in nature and training, 106.
,, perfection of, unites body, passions, intelligence, 8.
,, worth and power of, a better study than their opposites, 119.
Mausolus, 27.
Mechanical work, distress of, due to failure and degradation, 109.
,, ,, inconsistent with nobleness of race, *ib.*
,, ,, Dante, Shakspeare, and Homer on, *ib. n.*
,, ,, See s. βαναυσία.
Medicine, the economy of, 18.
Mens sana in corpore sano, the true doctrine, 6.
Merchants, agents of exchange, not to look for large profits, 98.
Mercy and merces, 100.
Meristic law fixes what all should and do possess, 114.
Merit, a better study than demerit, 119.
Mill, J. S., "Political Economy," quoted :—
    def. of wealth, *pref.* 1.
    on currency, Book iii. cap. 7, 77 *n.*
Milton, inferior to Homer and Dante, 87.
    Quoted :—
    "Thrones, Dominations, &c.," 105.
Mines, criminals to work in the, 159.
,, to be made safe, 159.
Misery of the poor, a national disgrace, 108.
Molyneux (Rev. —), on parable of the prodigal son, App. V.
Monarchy and tyranny, 133.
,, compared to a ship, republic to a raft, 124 *n.*
Money, accumulation of, is not political economy, 4.
,, ,, its temptations, 85-6.
,, credit-power of, 58 and *n.*
,, defined, a documentary legal claim to wealth, 21.
,, ill-gotten, ill spent, 86.
,, its enjoyment, secure and solitary, 85.
,, its study, 11.
,, love of, founded on a desire for things, 65 *n.*

INDEX.

Money, modern greed of, 153.
,, love of, inconsistent with high moral training, 108,
,, -making, men to stop when they have enough, 153.
,, possessor of much, generally has no fixed tastes, 85.
,, property and, which the end, which the means? 83.
,, to be spent by those who make it, 153.
,, value of, how affected, 58.
,, ,, altered by change in national character, and why, 65.
,, ,, changes in, 22 seq.
,, ought not to be intrinsically valuable with civilized people, 25.
,, is not wealth, 21, 36. See s. *Currency.*
Museums, free to be established, 115.

NAPOLEON I. on usury, 98.
Nations, divisible into lordly and servile classes, 109.
,, government and, correlatively noble, 122.
,, happiness of, not dependent on its numbers, 3.
National character, how indicated (its customs), 106.
,, ,, individual influences on, 122.
,, credit, to pay ready money like individuals, 38 *n.*
,, debt and national store, *pref.* seq. 18 seqq.
,, ,, does it enrich a nation, *pref.* 15, 18.
,, ,, would the discovery of a mountain of gold efface it? 76.
,, economy, on what dependent, 54.
,, expenditure and taxation, right objects of, 156.
,, health, compared to a great lake or sea, 109 *n.*
,, loss, explained, 155 *n.*
,, store and wealth, 40, 44.
,, ,, its nature and holders, 46 seq.
,, ,, and population, 54.
,, training, high, what it implies, 108.
National gallery, a treasury, not a school, of art, 115.
Nightingale's song "Domine Labia," 149 *n.*

OLIGARCHY, 123.
Orinoco, 37.

Pall Mall Gazette, Oct. 27, 1871 (Jules Simon on Paris), xviii. 16.
Paris, siege of, referred to, ix. 6.
,, ,, relief of, 1871 committee, xii. 10.
Parliament, Houses of, waste of labour, 157.
Pay, amount of, asked for by the best men, is small, 60 *n.* (*orig. ess.*).
,, and profit distinct, 98 *n.*
,, work that will not pay in money, but in life, 160.

Peace, grace essential to, 100.
Pelicans and climbing perch, 126.
Philotimé. See s. *Spenser*.
Phlegethon, sands of, 79.
Plato's enigmas, 87.
,, distrust of Homer, 87.
,, imagination quenched by his reason, 87.
,, political economy of, 2.
,, Sirens in, 90.
,, usury in, 98.
,, quoted, "Laws," Book 1, on Plutus, 88.
,, ,, ,, ,, 2, on choirs, dancing, &c., 102 *n*.
,, ,, ,, ,, 5, on money, 153 *n*.
,, ,, "Republic," the slave who wants to marry his master's daughter, 134.
,, ,, ,, Book 2, ὑῶν πόλις, 91.
,, ,, ,, ,, 3, on money, 89.
,, ,, ,, ,, 4, on political evils and their remedies, 98.
,, ,, ,, ,, 6 seq., on mechanical labour, 109 *n*.
Plinlimmon, plant with larch, 149.
Plutus, god of riches, blind, in Plato, Dante, Spenser, and Goethe, and in Dante, dumb, 88, A. I. (*orig. ess.*).
Poets, the great, speak in enigmas, 87.
,, ,, their *visionary* language about great truths deprecated, 87.
Political Economy, modern, described, 2.
,, ,, ,, faith in, tested, 128.
,, ,, ,, does not deal with national dress, rent, debt, &c., *pref.* 15.
,, ,, ,, looks only at the *exchange* value of wealth, *pref.* 7.
,, ,, ,, has never dealt with intrinsic value, *pref.* 8.
,, ,, ,, fallacy that labour is a saleable commodity, 59.
,, ,, ,, in America, 124.
,, ,, true, defined, *pref.* 1, 13.
,, ,, ,, does not give sentiment for science, *pref.* 13.
,, ,, ,, ethical postulates of, *pref.* 13, 81, 84.
,, ,, ,, founded on industry, frugality, and discretion, *pref.* 13.
,, ,, ,, knowledge of fine arts necessary to, *pref.* 1.
,, ,, ,, its end, to multiply noble life, not money, 4, 7.

INDEX. 235

Political Economy, true, not concerned with varying worth of bullion, 25.
,, ,, ,, to examine *moral* results of the laws of wealth, *pref.* 21.
,, ,, ,, to maintain a relation between supply and demand, *pref.* 11.
, ,, See s. *Author* (*Books*, "*Munera Pulveris*"), *Bacon, Books, Capital, Capitalists, Cheapness, Commerce, Competition, Cost, Credit, Currency, Demand, Dishonesty, Dress, Employment, Exchange, Expenditure, Fawcett, Finance, Free-trade, Funds, Gold, Labour, Land, Loans, Luxury, Mechanical Work, Merchants, Mill (J. S.), Money, National Character, Possession, Poverty, Price, Production, Profit, Property, Rich, Riches, Supply, Use, Usury, Value, Wages, War, Wealth, Worth.*
Political evils, the remedy for, in change of character, not of laws, 98.
Poor, the, directed by the rich, 29.
,, ,, governed by the rich, 146.
,, ,, number of, in relation to the rich, 138.
Pope, quoted :—
    "For forms of government," &c., 125.
    Epistle to Lord Bathurst, on currency, 77 *n*.
Population, extent of, in relation to national store, 54.
,, ,, ,, wealth, 55.
Portion, words connected with, 101 *n*.
Possession, defined, the legal right to keep what you have worked for, 141 and *n*.
,, guardianship and, distinct, 37.
,, useless without use, 37.
Poverty, always criminal, English doctrine, 136 *n*.
,, merely relative, 26.
,, wretched and blessed, 56 *n*.
Price, defined, 62 *n*.
,, is cost, if demand be constant, 63.
,, on what dependent (human will), 62.
,, one just value and, for everything, 62 *n*.
Production, ease of, only valuable so far as it enables the maintenance of more population, 62 *n*.
Profit, none, in true commerce, 99.
Property, fivefold, power over, 37.
,, money and, which the end, and which the means? 83.
,, security of, the first end of law, 67.
Punishment, true, in hindrance, 120 *n*.

Pyramid of gold may be worthless, 4.
Pyrrhon's answer, 132.

RACE, faculties dependent on, 106.
Railways, companies are turnpike keepers, 128.
,,   excursion trains, government control of, 157.
,,   quadruple lines needed, 128.
,,   trains, 157.
,,   station architecture, 128.
Recreate, force of the word, 9.
Religion, plain speaking on, objected to, 101 *n*.
Rent, does a landtax enrich a nation? *pref.* 15, 17.
Republic compared to a raft (Emerson), 124.
,,   distinct from democracy, 124.
,,   res publica and privata, 124.
Reverence, instinctive, just, and true reward, 120-1.
Revolution, how caused, 109 *n*.
Reward, true, is at once a help and a crown, 120 *n*.
Rich direct the poor, 29.
,,   govern the poor, 146.
,,   relation to poor, 136 seq.
Riches, does the mode of their distribution affect their nature, 27.
,,   of one man involve the subjection of others, 145.
,,   relativity of, 26.
,,   selection, direction, and provision, 29.
,,   their study, 11.
,,   to be collected and administered by economists, 27, 29.
Right, a man's, defined, 118.
,,   and wrong are life and death to man, 9.
Royal means right doing, 113.

ST. JOHN'S locusts, 130.
Sale is not commerce, 99.
Savings, the use of a man's, 152. See s. *Death.*
School, true meaning of, 109 *n*.
Scorpion whips, our pleasant vices, 130.
Scylla and Charybdis, meaning of, 93.
Sensibility defined, 106.
Servants, all who work for pay are, 145.
Shakspeare, his dreams, divine shadows of true facts, 134.
,,   speaks in enigmas, 87.
,,   the leader of English intellect, 100.
,,   his scorn of the populace, on what based, 109 *n*.
,,   his nomenclature, 100 *n*. 134 *n*.
,,   ,,   ,,   Greek names, 100 *n*. 134 *n*.
    Referred to :—
        Cymbeline, Iachimo, meaning of name, 134 *n*.
        ,,   Leonatus, 134 *n*.
        ,,   moral of, 134 *n*.

Shakspeare, quoted, *continued* :—
    Hamlet, meaning of the name (home), 134 *n.*
    ,,   Ophelia = serviceableness, 134 *n.*
    ,,   quoted, "A ministering angel," &c. 134 *n.*
    ,,   ,,   "Herb o' grace o' Sundays," App. VI.
    King Lear, Cordelia = heart-lady, 100 *n.*
        quoted :
            v. 3. "our pleasant vices . . . scourge us."
    Merchant of Venice, its lesson, 100.
    ,,   ,,   meaning of, 134.
    ,,   ,,   Portia = portion, 100 and *n.*
    ,,   ,,   Antonio, nobility of, 100.
    ,,   ,,   Shylock, 100.
    Much Ado about Nothing, Beatrice, meaning of, 134 *n.*
    ,,   ,,   Benedict, meaning of, 134 *n.*
    Othello, catastrophe of, how caused, 134 *n.*
    ,,   meaning of name, 134 *n.*
    ,,   Desdemona, meaning of, 134 *n.*
    ,,   Iago, meaning of, 134 *n.*
    Tempest, analysis of, 134 seq.
    ,,   Ariel = generous faithful service, 133-4.
    ,,   Caliban, 133-4.
    ,,   ,,   and slavery and freedom, 133-4.
    ,,   Miranda "the wonderful," 134.
    ,,   Prospero = hope, 134.
    ,,   Sycorax = swine-raven, 134 and *n.*
    ,,   quoted :
        dew brushed with raven's feather, 134.
        incensed seas and shores, 134.
        put a girdle round the earth, 134.
        fetches dew . . . asleep, 134.
        thought is free, 134.
        full fathom, &c., 134.
        come unto these yellow sands, 134.
        "courtesied," 134.
        all but mariners, 134.
        with bemocked-at, &c., 134.
        where the bee sucks, 134.
        side stitches, &c., 134.
        that's a brave god, &c., 134.
    Two Gentlemen of Verona, Proteus, name, 134 *n.*
    ,,   ,,   Valentine, name, 134 *n.*
    Winter's Tale, Hermione, name, 134 *n.*
    ,,   ,,   Perdita = lost lady, 134 *n.*

Ships, English, with defences *v.* liquid fire, 127.
Sirens or pleasures, Bacon's view of, 90.
  ,,   ,,   are really desires, 90.
  ,,   and Circe, distinct, 92.
  ,,   their destructive power, 92.
Sillar, W. C., on usury, 98 and *n.*
Simon, M. Jules, on Paris, xviii. 16.
Slavery, American and English methods of, 131.
  ,,   modern, examples of, 124 *n.*

Slavery, not a political institution, 133.
,, right and wrong, considered, 130 seq.
,, true nature of, in its cramping, 134.
Socialism, modern, *pref.* 21.
Soldiers, men are ready to die, but not to spend money for their country, 148.
Soul and body, not really opposed, 6.
Speculation = peculation, 79.
,, evils of, 153 *n.*
Spenser quoted, 93.
,, his Philotimé, 93.
,, ,, Plutus, 88.
Splendour of living, what it involves to others, 145.
Sport, shooting of birds, 149.
State, maintenance of a, defined, 3.
Steam-agriculture, 149.
,, -power, its true use, 159.
Store, national, in relation to the currency, 81 seq.
Stork and frogs, fable of, and tyranny, 126.
Streams, not to be defiled, 115.
Success, under competition, its meaning, 139.
Supply and demand, fallacy of (siege of Paris), *pref.* 9 seq.
,, ,, results of (Paris print-shops), viii. 4.
,, ,, doctrine, 124.

TAXATION, currencies may be disguised, 78.
Tennant, Sir Emerson, "Ceylon" quoted, 126.
Times, June 4, 1862, on killing of birds, 149 *n.*
,, Dec. 25, 1862, on modern civilization and revolution, 108 *n.*
,, Feb. 4, 1863, on average earnings of the poor, 124 *n.*
Tintoret, author's estimate of, 1851-71, *pref.* 4.
,, pictures of, and Paris lithographs, *pref.* 5.
,, ,, in shreds, S. Rocco, 1851, *pref.* 3.
Tisiphone, the rule of, 130.
Tobacco, 65 *n.*
Trade has come to mean = fraud, 99.
,, meaning of word, and traitor, 99.
Tradesmen are the servants of their customers, 145.
Trionfo della Morte, 48.
Trust, meaning of the word, 81 (*orig. ess. n.*).
Truths, the great poets veil their greatest, in enigma, 87.
Tyranny, illustrated by fable of frogs and stork, 126.
,, and monarchy, 123.

ULYSSES, Dante on death of, 93.
,, and the Sirens, their appeal to his vanity, 92.
Use, possession without, is valueless, 37.
,, power of, essential to wealth, 37.

INDEX. 239

Useful and useless, defined, 8.
Usury, abolition of, by purifying national character, 98.
,,   author's first notes on, 148 *n.* 41 (*orig. ess.*).
,,   Dante on, 88.
,,   essence and evil of, 98 and *n.*
,,   French economists on, 148 *n.*
,,   Greek and mediæval horror of, 98 *n.*
,,   Plato, Bacon, and Napoleon I. on, 98.
,,   Shakspeare on ("Merchant of Venice"), 100.

VALUE, definition of, 12 seq.
,,   distinct from cost or price, 12.
,,   effectual, defined, and wealth and currency, 39.
,,   ,,   depends on use, and power to use, 14.
,,   international, 96 *n.*
,,   intrinsic, at base of true political economy, *pref.* 8-9.
,,   ,,   and effectual, 12 seq.
,,   ,,   worth makes value, not demand or money, 31.
,,   just, everything has its, 62.
,,   list of things of, 15.
Venice, coinage of, pure, 75 *n.* 77 *n.*
,,   S. Rocco, Tintorets there in shreds, 1851, 3.
Vices, our pleasant, scorpion whips, 130.
Virgil, Tityre tu patulæ, &c., 149.
,,   quæ maxima turba, 88.
Virtues, the four cardinal, App. I.
Visions of great poets on great truths, 87.
Volunteer labour, objects of, proposed, 149.
,,   movement, to be extended beyond war, 149.
Votes, number of a man's votes to be increased with his age, &c., 129.

WAGES, competition not to determine, *pref.* 12.
,,   defined by modern political economy as "the sum which will maintain the labourer," 136.
,,   equality of, depends on moral conditions, 137.
,,   principles of, illustrated by story of inundation, 141.
War, cheap, proposed, 128.
,,   fostered by capitalists to make investments, *pref.* 19.
,,   idleness of upper classes, a cause of, 149 *n.*
,,   ill-accumulated money spent in, 86.
,,   the necessity of, amongst unjust persons only, A. II.
Wealth, attainment of great, impossible by one man, 139.
,,   ,,   modern trickery of, *pref.* 13.
,,   ,,   wish to die rich, 153.
,,   caprice will not make a thing, 35.
,,   defined, 11 seq.
,,   ,,   as "a thing of value in the hands of those who can use it" (valuable and valiant), 14.

Wealth defined, "intrinsic value developed by vital power," 31.
,,   ,,   "the constant objects of right desire," 34.
,,   ,,   Mill's definition criticised, *pref.* 1.
,,   ,,   few people realise what true wealth is, *pref.* 2.
,,   desire of, true wealth is moderately desired, *pref.* 21.
,,   effectual value, and, 39
,,   exchangeability, and distinct, 35.
,,   luxury and, see s. *Luxury.*
,,   money, and distinct, 36.
,,   national wealth not only in amount, but in the power to use it, 27 *n.*
,,   national character, its importance to the distribution of wealth, 84.
,,   the phantasm of, 38.
,,   the possession of, who are the possessors of wealth, is nationally more important than its amount 84.
,,   its possession always conditional, 115.
,,   to be the reward of sagacity and work, 129.
,,   the saving up of, 153.
Whewell, Dr., on usury, 148 *n.*
Wine, English expenditure in, why no word "oino-maniac," 65.
Wise, John R., on meaning of Sycorax (see Shakspeare), 134 *n.*
Words, accurate use of, by great thinkers, 2.
,,   derivation of, App. VI.
,,   first meaning of, often the truest, 2.
Work, good, to be got by willingness, not money, 50 *n.*
,,   wise or foolish, results in life or death, 10.
Worth, the recognition of, in others, to be sought after, 121.
,,   ,,   the first thing in a nation, 121.
,,   of things, not dependent on price, *pref.* 7.

XENOPHON's Political Economy, 2.
,,   Economist, on βαναυσία, 109 *n.*
,,   ,,   on wealth and use, App. III.
,,   Memorabilia, Book II. on grace and equity, 100.

ZECCHIN, pure gold of Venetian, 77 *n.*

THE END.

Printed by BALLANTYNE, HANSON & Co.
Edinburgh and London

www.ingramcontent.com/pod-product-compliance
Lightning Source LLC
Chambersburg PA
CBHW031252250426
43672CB00029BA/2114